GIANT KILLER

GIANT KILLER

Winning the Battles That Matter Most

JON PEACOCK AND BLAKE WILLIAMS

BOOKLOGIX˙

Alpharetta, GA

ISBN: 978-1-6653-0393-4 - Paperback

eISBN: 978-1-6653-0394-1 - eBook

051922

READ THIS FIRST

HOW DO YOU cowrite a book? We weren't sure either, but we've enjoyed the process. Let's first begin by introducing ourselves.

BLAKE'S STORY

My name is Blake, and I am a Giant Killer.

I wasn't always—and of course, there are times when I still fall short—but yeah, I've slain my fair share of giants. The path I traveled to become a Giant Killer is not one I wish for others. There is a better way, which Jon and I will unwrap in this book. But regardless of the path we take to get there, our end goal is the same—to live a victorious life.

It's been said before that "you only live once, but if you do it right, once is enough."

I agree wholeheartedly that living life "right" is living a life of victory. A victorious life offers good to others and glory to God.

Born and raised in Alabama, I started facing giants right out of the womb. I won't go into all the details, but my birth family was extremely dysfunctional, stemming from generations of dysfunction before them. The family shattered when I was three and was never pieced back together. My mom and two older sisters moved to Florida, and my older brother and I moved to Talladega, Alabama, to live with my great-aunt and great-grandmother. Our paths would seldom cross until I graduated from college. My father was in and out of jail when I was young and simply chose to be absent when he wasn't behind bars.

The feeling that I had been abandoned haunted me as I grew. It made me feel flawed, unloved, and extremely insecure in who I was. As a result, fear and self-doubt have been the giants I've faced on a regular basis. I've felt like a victim for much of my life. *Why did those things have to happen to me?* was my thinking. I felt like the world owed me something but was unsure if it would ever pay up.

I've learned more about the victorious life in times of war than in times of peace. I've learned from the battles of life and, in many ways, they have become my greatest teacher. These days, I win a lot more often than I lose. I no longer live like a victim. I fully believe life happens *for* me, not *to* me.

Ten years ago, I founded a non-profit called Battle-Tested. We help prepare the next generation for the battles they will face in life. And we do that primarily by serving high school and college sports teams through team building, leadership development, and character development. Battle-Tested has provided me with many opportunities to face and fight giants—giants that tried to prevent me from starting the company, and the many that have tried to slow me down along the way.

In the past year, I've become a single dad to five amazing kids. More on this later, but Everley, Finley, Hudson, Hadley, and Cooper, I love you deeply. Beauty will come from these ashes. If this book encourages and equips anyone, I hope it's you five—you are Giant Killers.

Here's what I know: The wins and losses I've experienced have equipped me to equip YOU.

If you want to kill giants, I'm here to help.

JON'S STORY

My name is Jon, I'm forty-two years old, I'm Blake's biggest fan, I enjoy long walks on the beach—oh, and I'm a Giant Killer.

My story is very different from Blake's. Very. I learned how to slay giants from my dad, mom, and two older brothers. I'm forever grateful for the home I was raised in and the family I deeply enjoy to this day. My journey of facing giants began first with giant awareness. Yes, "giant awareness" is a term we've made up but let's agree, awareness is where anything of significance begins. Some of you are sufficiently aware of your giants. Others of you are about to be.

The first three decades of my life were not filled with loss, but with ease. The abundance of love in my home and the abundance of success as an athlete growing up and in college at a D1 level school are things I am grateful for—I truly am. I'll have those memories forever. That said, for most of my life, things have come easily. What I didn't know was that ease had a cost.

Denzel said, "Ease is a greater threat to progress than

hardship." He's right, and before I go *Remember the Titans* on you, let me be upfront: there is a giant standing before you, and in my humble opinion, it's time for him to fall.

Will it be easy? No.

Will it be worth it? Yes.

In the pages that follow, I will share with you, from experience, what I've learned over the past ten years of church planting. What started with just a handful of people in my house is now something to behold. There's a whole bunch of us helping people find and follow Christ in a lovely place we call The 10. More on this later, but let's just say that in 2011, my life of ease was replaced with a life of anything but, and I thank God for that. I have faced challenge after challenge and, oddly enough, as I look back I am deeply grateful for the crucible church planting has become.

I've learned a lot over the past decade.

I've learned there is nothing better than doing a great life's work in a circle of great friends. Mission Staff and Mission Lead Team, that's you!

I've learned I'm at my best when I have a coach. KB, that's you!

I've learned you only keep what you give away. That's why I now coach others. Coaching Cohort, that's you!

I've learned there's nothing greater than a wonderful wife. KP, that's you!

I've learned there is nothing stronger than a three-legged stool. Tommy and Dan, that's us! Where would I be without you two?! Don't answer that.

I've learned times of war are better teachers than times of peace.

Lastly, and most importantly, I've learned this: **Jesus is the David for my Giant**. If I introduce you to one truth, may that be the one. Jesus Christ is how and why I live *FROM* victory and *FOR* victory.

I'm confident of this: Some of you instantly connect with Blake's story because you've experienced something similar. There is no one I know more familiar with loss and setbacks than Blake. Others, you connect more with my story. Someone killed the bear and lion for you and yet now you've started something (a business, a family, or a church) or have taken over something and feel anything but ready for the battle at hand.

Bottom line: If you want to become battle-ready, I'm here to help.

In the summer of 2021, we had the idea of putting together a book we could hand folks who are facing difficulty. As we ate breakfast that day, we dreamed. We thought, *How great would it be if we could help folks like us, who have tasted both victory and defeat? How amazing would it be if we could help them taste victory a whole lot more than they taste defeat?* We then thought of teams: both corporate teams and athletic teams. We thought about how dynamic teams *could* be if they had more Giant Killers sitting around the table.

Here's our agenda: We want to add value to your life, family, career, and community. We're showing our cards upfront.

READ THIS SECOND

WE WILL WRITE the remainder of this book as one voice. Some parts will include stories where we might clarify who it is that's writing, but you can be sure of this: we've labored together over EVERY. SINGLE. WORD.

Why?

Every word matters. We are asking God to turn each word into a weapon that causes you to experience more and more of the victorious life.

Before we describe the giants we face, we want to first explain our **Five-Step Process for Killing Giants**. If content is not actionable, we're not interested! Throughout the book when these steps appear, we will use *S1, S2, S3, S4,* and *S5* as shorthand for each step. You'll catch on. This five-step process is helpful in coaching employees, raising kids, and leading yourself. The shorthand helps us ask the question, *What step is most important now?* That said, who doesn't love a good five-step plan? This section would make John Maxwell smile. We hope so, at least.

> *Give me six hours to chop down a tree and I will spend the first four sharpening my axe.*
>
> —Abraham Lincoln

We might only get an hour of your time so we feel it necessary to start by sharpening the axe of your understanding on how one might chop down a giant.

The answer? One step at a time.

Before we lay out the five steps, let's get clear on this: we all face giants in our lives. Welcome to being a human. Many giants are enormous and terrifying (think: Goliath). At the same time, some of life's greatest giants specialize in subtly. They are insidious. Think of a tick. If you know anyone with Lyme disease, they will tell you how something so tiny has caused so much pain and difficulty. Whether macro or micro, giants yield mega pain and wreckage in one's life.

Some giants are born from circumstances beyond our control. We simply wake up one day and there's a giant waiting outside our bedroom door. Perhaps a traumatic event has happened and you're left facing a giant. Other giants, we fabricate ourselves, perhaps from wounds we've endured in life. And since the wound occurred, we've been battling a particular giant ever since. We may be successful at beating the giant back at times and, therefore, experience some periods of relief, but he's still there, day in and day out.

We're not sure of your past but we are certain of your future: giants will come. The question is, will giants fall?

We know you know this, but we have to say it—before a giant falls, a giant is FACED. A legendary Giant Killer from Bethlehem was a shepherd by the name of David—the youngest of eight boys, he is best known as King David. This shepherd-king is, of course, the most famous of Giant Killers in the Bible. Even if you were not raised in a church or have never picked up the Bible before, you've heard the story of the ginormous man named Goliath and the small shepherd boy named David. This story has become the go-to story in pregame speeches for coaches around the world. Raise your hand if you've been on the receiving end of a coach calling the opposing team Goliath and you David. Our hands are raised as well.

We may not all believe in God, but we all believe in giants. Outlined in this book, we will discuss some of the fiercest giants known to mankind: the Giant of Fear, Anxiety, Comfort, Self-doubt, Temptation, Pride, and lastly, the Giant of Loss.

Let us say it again: giants will come. The question is, will giants fall?

As mentioned before, there are five steps to killing giants, and Step 1 is: **Decide**.

STEP 1 (S1): DECIDE

AS FOR THE giant named Goliath, a **decision** preceded his death. David decided to *face* the giant. Think about that. It's easy to quickly move past this first step, but Step 1 may be the most important of all. If you have a highlighter, get it out and highlight this next sentence. If you want to **fell some giants**, you must make the conscious choice to **face some giants.**

You cannot outsource this decision. You and only *you* must **decide!**

There is no point in reading any further unless you first decide to engage in the fight.

As you think about your decision, let us say this: David had no idea how significant his decision to engage would be; it was his inciting incident. Awaiting him on the other side of his decision was a brand-new life. David would go from anonymity to celebrity. He would go from the forgotten eighth son to the never-forgotten King of Israel. The rest of the army was blessed that day and yet only one person had decided. That's what decisions do. Hundreds decided *not* to fight yet still received the blessing because of the one that decided *to* fight.

The same is true in your life. There are lives around you right now that will be forever impacted by your choice to engage in this fight. Your *yes* will *bless* those around you.

Your decision will have a direct impact on those you love most: your spouse, your roommate, your coworkers, your parents, your church, your team, your boss, your community, your country, your children, and grandchildren. Your choice to engage could even impact the generations that follow you. It did for David; it will for you. Get this: brain science now proves thought patterns, whether healthy or unhealthy, are passed down to the *fourth generation*!

If you're looking to give a gift to the generations that follow, how about giving them the gift of a thought pattern that chose to engage in the battles that matter most.

Decide to Engage.

STEP 2 (S2): DISCERN

YOU MUST KNOW who you are fighting. Your strategy toward victory will be in direct correlation to discerning who it is you are fighting. Am I stepping into the ring with Mike Tyson or Sugar Ray?

For example, the Giant of Fear is defeated differently than the Giant of Temptation.

Giant Killers **learn** to **discern**.

Anyone who has ever engaged in battle knows the most dangerous enemy is the one you are unaware of. As mentioned previously, we call this "giant awareness." The more we discern *who* the giant is, the more our chances of winning the battle increase. This is why football coaches spend an inordinate amount of time studying film. Why Moses sent spies to scope out the land before they did anything else. Why Jason Bourne will always be employed—and for the fact that he can't be killed, but you get the point. **Decide then Discern!**

In the chapters that follow, we will do our very best to get granular with each giant. In the movie *Hoosiers*, the great Norman Dale (played by Gene Hackman) said, *"Stick with your man. Think of him as chewing gum. By the end of the game, I want you to know what flavor he is."*

By the end of this book, you will know what flavor your giant is.

STEP 3 (S3): DISCOVER

ONCE WE DISCERN who we're fighting, we then **discover** what weapon is most helpful in defeating that enemy. Think *strategy* here. If you grew up playing *Contra*, think back to when you needed the fireball gun instead of the spread gun. That's when you first learned "strategery."

While we're here, let's just add this: up, up, down, down, left, right, left, right, B, A, start!

We've looked into this and the bad news is there are no cheat codes for the actual battles in life. The good news? Like David, we can discover the appropriate weapon for the battle at hand. At times, a shepherd used a staff or club; other times, they used a sling.

1 Samuel 17:40 (NIV) tells us, *"Then he [David] took his staff in his hand, chose five smooth stones from the stream, put them in the pouch of his shepherd's bag and, with his sling in his hand, approached the Philistine."*

There is one thing here we want to make sure you don't miss: David discovered the best strategy to defeat Goliath (think: sling and stone). In each section, we will offer a *sling and stone* approach to each giant by highlighting and explaining what we consider a *keystone strategy*. Similar to a keystone habit, keystone strategies are more catalytic than other strategies. David could have chosen the strategy of the sword and that would have been a good choice, but not the best choice. The best choice was the sling and stone. Before we misunderstand this weapon of choice as cute or novel, understand this: slingers in David's day released stones at speeds of two hundred miles per hour! These deadly weapons boasted the stopping power on par with a bullet shot from a .45 caliber pistol.

In his book *David and Goliath: Underdogs, Misfits, and the Art of Battling Giants*, author Malcolm Gladwell writes that experienced slingers could kill a target of up to two hundred yards or even kill a bird in flight. David chose the correct strategy for the giant at hand. Big and slow was no match for agility and speed, and David knew it.

The discovery step (S3) is critical for every Giant Killer.

STEP 4 (S4): DEVELOP

DAVID WAS NOT an overnight success, you know why? Because there is no such thing as an overnight success. The navy SEALs said it best: *"Under pressure, you don't rise to the occasion, you sink to the level of your own training."*

That's exactly what happened. This multi-year overnight success named David honed his craft by developing it over and over again. Like Rocky, he trained. He chased his chickens. He put in his ten thousand hours when no one was watching, and it paid off when everyone *was* watching. This shepherd became a stone-cold STONE SLINGER! David didn't know it at the time, but tending his father's sheep—and subsequently killing a bear and a lion—would help prepare him to fight and win the greatest battle of his young life.

Step 4 fires us up! We need to fall in love with the process of development. In his must-read book *Atomic Habits*, author James Clear writes, *"Winners and losers have the same goals . . . Ultimately, it is your commitment to the process that will determine your progress."*

In the words of Coach Saban, one of the greatest coaches of all time, *"Trust the process."*

In the words of Robert Louis Stevenson, *"Don't judge each day by the harvest you reap but by the seeds that you plant."*

This is why, at the height of his career, Tiger Woods made one thousand putts a day. Why Steph Curry, the best shooter of all time, makes five hundred shots a day! Why Kobe got to the gym at four a.m. That's commitment to the process!

Highlight this: Giant Killers *do the work*! They plant seeds by developing strategies for victory. They fall in love with the process. They don't get caught up in early returns, they get caught up in lasting victory, and that victory only comes through skill development. They go the extra mile. They make the extra putt. They run the extra lap. They rehearse the presentation. They embrace the reality that skill development is like compounding interest.

Here's the principle: The best strategy in the world is worthless if not developed. Make no mistake, David was unknown, but he was not undeveloped.

STEP 5 (S5): DEPLOY

ARROWS ARE MEANT to be released. Developed skills are meant to be **deployed**. Step 5 is when we take aim and release the skill we have developed, in the direction of our enemy. This is where our paralleling with David and Goliath parts ways. For David, it was a single stone. For your giant, it will require many more.

We wish taking down the Giant of Fear required one decisive act of courage, but the truth is, our giants have the tendency of getting back up. As we develop skills for taking down giants, we form practices that can be repeated. For some, you may experience the sheer thrill of forever slaying your giant. If that's you, we praise God for that. For others, you will be given the opportunity of skill deployment over and over again.

As you can see in the diagram, our Five-Step Process for Killing Giants is not linear, but cyclical. We work these steps repeatedly. Getting a victory is one thing, staying victorious is something else altogether.

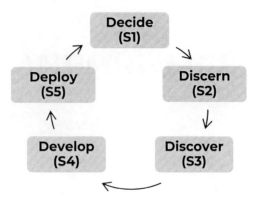

If you fast forward in the story of David, you'll learn it would have served him quite well to return to Step 1. Instead, in another time of war, David did not **decide**. He opted out. Has this part of his story ever stood out to you? It should. David stayed back and it cost him—greatly. We'll explore that part of his story later.

For the Giant Killer, there are no off days, vacations, or times of peace from the giants of life. In the words of David Goggins, *"Stay hard,"* meaning keep your heart and soul engaged in the fight. In one phrase: DECIDE DAILY!

If you are familiar with the story of David and Goliath, you know there are many other stories taking place at the same time. One of those stories is of the Israelite Army, there was a group of men who failed Step 1. They did not **decide**.

Here's our take on how it went down:

The Israelite Army gathered in small groups—let's call them Soldier Small Groups. Your church has them, your business has a version of these, as well as your team or school.

As for the Soldier Small Groups, I imagined they had discussions like this:

"Guys, Goliath is out there again!"

Another guy speaks up, "Why does Goliath keep coming back every day? Will he ever take a break? Ugh!"

Someone from the back blurts out, "Why doesn't God do something about this?"

And then—get this—a new guy to Solider Small Group says, "Hey, guys, I'm new and I don't know how all this works but what if we did something about this?"

After an awkward silence, the group bursts into laughter. Doubling over from laughing, the Soldier Small Group leader says, with tears rolling down his face, "We . . . us . . . no. C'mon, new guy, that's not what this group is about. We don't commit to actually doing something, we gather as a group to talk about what life could be like if, one day, we actually did something."

So they decide to circle up again and again at Solider Small Group, week after week, and talk about how they should do something about this giant who is taking their lunch money, but you guessed it, nobody does a thing!

Nothing. Zero. Zilch.

We just explained what many have accepted as life. It's not only tragic but also untrue. What we just described is not living, it's existing.

Many choose to live life so close to victory yet settle for defeat week in and week out.

Not you. Not anymore. This book is for those who are ready to no longer confuse circling up with throwing down.

For the love of God, for the love of family, for the love of country: **Decide to Engage!**

It's time to unleash some haymakers. It's time to slay some giants.

Section One

_____

THE GIANT
OF FEAR

The brave man is not he who does not feel afraid, but he who conquers that fear.

—Nelson Mandela

DISCERN FEAR (S2)

THERE IS A giant and his name is **FEAR**.

He's often camouflaged as caution, safety, or "thinking it through," but make no mistake we are swimming in a sea of fear.

Perhaps you've heard, the twenty-first century is now being called the Age of Fear. Every direction we look, we find fear:

Fear of change; fear of not enough change.

Fear of being too much; fear of not being enough.

Fear of starting; fear of stopping.

Fear of not building something; fear of losing what we've built.

Fear of getting hurt; fear of getting hurt again.

Crude oil is not the number one commodity in the world — fear is. And look at what it's yielding!

Fear is hijacking lives. It's unraveling homes and destroying health. Fear is polluting the culture of companies, teams, and families, and **we are letting it happen!**

We are and so were they—the fear of the Israelite Army had both a reputation and a name. His reputation was victory, his name was Goliath.

The story of David and Goliath is found in 1 Samuel 17. It begins with this detail: *"The Philistines occupied one hill and the Israelites another, with the **valley** between them"* (1 Samuel 17:3 (NIV)).

We love this detail because it vividly describes our lives and yours. No matter what year it is, no matter what age we are, there's **now** ground and there's **new** ground. It's true relationally and physically; it's true for your career and for your craft.

The **now** ground is where you are *now*.

The **new** ground is where you need to be *next*.

How inspiring to believe the best is yet to come. How encouraging to think new ground is in our future, or better said, *could be* in our future. However, before you start picking out carpet and paint colors for the new ground, we need to point out a critical detail found in that verse.

There was a **valley** between their now and their new, and there was someone occupying that valley, and that someone happened to be a giant named Goliath.

True for them. True for us. New ground will *always* be defended by a giant.

New ground isn't given, new ground is **taken**.

The next verse says, *"A champion named **Goliath**, who was from Gath, came out of the Philistine camp."*

This champion named Goliath stood nine feet, six inches

tall. The tip of his javelin spear alone weighed fifteen pounds while his armored coat weighed 125 pounds. Read that again.

To help you understand the capacity of this champion, Goliath was pretty much a nine-foot, six-inch Chuck Norris, and like Norris, Goliath could make onions cry.

Goliath stood between the now ground and the new ground and was not quiet about it. No, he began to run his mouth like most giants do.

Goliath said, *"Choose a man and have him come down to me. If he is able to fight and kill me, we will become your subjects; but if I overcome him and kill him, you will become our subjects and serve us"* (1 Samuel 17:8-9 (NIV)).

The response? Crickets. Instead of advancing in **courage**, they froze in **fear**.

The story goes on to reveal, *"For **forty days** the Philistine came forward **every morning** and **evening** and took his stand"* (1 Samuel 17:16 (NIV)).

For forty days! Why does this detail matter? Their giant wouldn't go away and neither will yours.

Forty days, both morning and night, which adds up to **eighty times**, Goliath taunted the army of Israel. Goliath was massive the first time he appeared, but by the eightieth time, he must have looked like a mountain.

Every Giant Killer has arrived at this conclusion: every day you choose to not **face** your fear, you **feed** your fear.

Choosing to not face our fear is what causes our fear to grow. The Israelites' giant, Goliath, didn't grow in forty days, but their fear did. This is why Step 1 of our five-step process is to **decide to engage**. Deciding to engage is mission-critical.

Years ago, I (Jon) went to Maui for a friend's bachelor party. Both me and Blake were on this trip. For some reason, our wives agreed to this crazy idea, and off we went. Our time was unforgettable—tons of laughter and tons of adventure. One of the best memories was cliff jumping at Ching's Pond on the road to Hana. We found some pretty good jumps and some "scare the crap out of you" jumps.

I learned two things that day:

1. Always let Blake go first, because he'll be glad to do so.
2. The longer you stand on the edge, the longer you stay on the edge.

Some of my friends, like Blake, never hesitated to jump. Me, on the other hand, I "needed" to evaluate the situation. I would say to the guys, "Fellas, I promised Kelly I'd return home unscathed," and so I stood there on the edge, blaming my wife while getting owned by fear. The result? What began as a forty-foot jump now felt like an eighty-foot jump.

Fear does that. Fear has done that. Fear is doing that.

Right now, you are standing on the edge of something. It's most likely not a cliff in Hawaii but it might be the edge of starting something or ending something. It could be the edge of fostering or adopting, or asking for someone's hand in marriage. Some of you are on the edge of applying for that job or graduate school. Some of you are standing on the edge of getting started or getting sober. Others are standing on the edge of restarting a department or reconciling a relationship. No matter what edge you're standing on, the longer you stand on the edge, the longer you'll stay on the edge.

For forty days, the Israelites stood on the edge, frozen in fear. The story says, *"Whenever the Israelites saw the man [Goliath], they all fled from him in great fear"* (1 Samuel 17:24 (NIV)).

A few years ago, I heard a friend of mine define fear as:

FEAR = False **E**vidence **A**ppearing **R**eal

Was the giant powerful? **Yes.** Was he all-powerful? **No.**

Was the giant strong? **Yes.** Was he without any weaknesses? **No.**

In his book *David and Goliath: Underdogs, Misfits, and the Art of Battling Giants*, Malcolm Gladwell says this of giants: *"Giants are not what we think they are. The same qualities that appear to give them strength are often the sources of great weakness."*

Gladwell goes on to explain how giants suffer from what is called *acromegaly*. This hormonal disorder develops when the pituitary gland produces too much growth hormone.

As you might expect, there are a lot of side effects but the one side effect that relates to this story is how acromegaly often causes impaired vision.

You can make the argument that Goliath, just like other giants, suffered from an inability to see as well as David. The evidence appearing real was that Goliath had no weaknesses but only strengths—and that evidence was simply false.

Being undefeated is not the same as being undefeatable.

This reality only one person knew. His name was David, a small shepherd boy who showed up not only in attendance, but in courage. You've heard how this story ends.

There in the valley, the giant fell.

There in the valley, courage triumphed over fear.

> *Being fearless isn't being 100 percent not fearful, it's being terrified but you jump anyway.*
>
> —Taylor Swift

Giant Killers *shake it off*, they walk up to the edge, and jump.

We all have a choice. Will we flee from fear, or will we face our fear? Will we stand on the edge, or will we jump?

DISCOVER COURAGE (S3)

MANY STRATEGIES ARE useful in fighting the Giant of Fear but few, if any, are more effective than courage.

John Wayne describes courage as *"being scared to death, but saddling up anyway."*

Band of Brothers is one of our all-time favorite mini-series. If you've seen it, you know it's a story chronicling the courage and indescribable sacrifice of those who fought and defeated a modern-day giant by the name of Hitler. What a victory that was!

In one episode, there's a scene of a conversation between two soldiers. One man is named Blithe, the other is Speirs. Albert Blithe was paralyzed by fear. For good reason, he lay in the bunker, frozen in fear. Speirs was known among the Battalion as the most courageous of all, and as the two shared a foxhole one night, Blithe asked Speirs, *"How are you so courageous. How?"* Spiers responded, *"Blithe, the only way forward is to accept the fact that you are already dead."*

Somewhere along the line, we began to confuse a long life with a great life. Don't get us wrong, we'd like to live to one hundred but not if that life is dominated and controlled by fear. We call that existing—not living. The *Speirs mindset* is supported by the Bible. It's the mindset of all the greats.

Jesus said, "*Whoever finds their life will lose it, and whoever loses their life for my sake will find it*" (Matthew 10:39 (NIV)).

The Apostle Paul echoes a very similar mindset in Galatians 2 where he says, "*I have been crucified with Christ and I no longer live, but Christ lives in me. The life I now live in the body, I live by faith in the Son of God, who loved me and gave himself for me*" (Galatians 2:20 (NIV)).

We know not everyone reading this book would consider themselves a follower of Jesus. If that is you, we want you to know one of the greatest advantages to surrendering your life to Jesus is you no longer have to be afraid.

The fear of rejection was handled the day you were welcomed into God's family.

The fear of failure was dealt with the day you realized you are loved by God. Period.

The fear of even death itself was overcome because Jesus overcame it. The grave is empty!

Winston Churchill once said, "*Success is not final, failure is not fatal: it is the courage to continue that counts.*"

If you are a Christian, that is *especially* true. We hope this section reminds you of one of the greatest advantages you have in this life: life *forever*. This is why courage and Christianity were synonymous in the first and second centuries. The ones who began the Christian faith did the math and arrived at the conclusion that life in eternity is a whole lot longer than life on earth.

Courage was their signature. Courage was their brand.

In April 2015, a small group of women set out to accomplish a world's first: to row a rowboat across the Pacific Ocean—from San Francisco, California, to Australia. Only one of the ladies had any rowing experience. Talk about some serious **S3**! Undeterred, they created a non-profit to raise money for women's charities and bought a big fancy rowboat—a twenty-nine-foot pink beauty they named *Doris*.

Doris had a sleeping cabin on one end (big enough for two) and on the other end was all the navigational and communications equipment necessary to guide them along the way and keep in touch with those back on the mainland. Down the middle of *Doris* was a single track with two seats and two sets of oars. Two ladies rowed the boat at a time, and each took two-hour shifts throughout the day.

Eleven days into their journey, they realized that *Doris* had a leak. The leak was in the compartment that housed the electronics. They had to return to land for repairs. The closest land to them was California, so they had to turn around and head back to the US. They landed in Santa Barbara on day sixteen, for repairs, and then were actually farther away from their destination than when they departed San Francisco. A great way to start the trip, right?

After repairs, the ladies set off again. Now, these ladies would have to make a couple of stops along the way to Australia in order to get more food and fresh water. Their first stop would be Hawaii. The team made it to Hawaii on day one hundred—they had rowed 2,759 miles at that point.

Their next stop would be the island of Samoa, but before arriving there, they would have to pass through the

Intertropical Convergence Zone, which is a stretch of water that encapsulates the equator. On the north side of the equator, the water current runs straight east, and on the south side of the equator, the current runs straight west.

Due to the current and the winds, there were times that the ladies were being pushed in the opposite direction of where they wanted to go. There were days when they were being pushed ten miles farther away from their destination. But there were also days when the winds and currents were in their favor, and they would cover as much as thirty miles in the right direction in a day. Sounds like life, right? Some good days and some not-so-good days.

They reached Samoa after 197 days, having rowed 5,430 miles. Due to winds and currents working against them along much of the route, they had to spend Christmas and New Year's on the boat in the middle of the ocean. They finally reached Australia after 257 days, having rowed 8,579 miles. What a feat!

The motto these ladies clung to for their journey was this, *"You can never cross the ocean until you have the courage to lose sight of the shore."*

Do like David. Head to the stream to discover your weapon.

If your giant is fear, courage is your stone!

DEVELOP COURAGE (S4)

IN THIS SECTION we'll highlight three strategies that will help you develop courage. Remember these strategies are things we practice over and over again to develop the skill of courage.

Some of you right now are thinking, *I don't have any good skills—you know, like nunchucks skills, bow-hunting skills, computer-hacking skills.*

Tell your inner Napoleon this: the skill of courage can be developed.

Courage, like making putts and jump shots, can be practiced repeatedly. Courage is the stone we discover *and* develop. Courage is both a strategy and a skill. The more courage we can develop (S4), the more courage we can deploy (S5).

Let's dispel a myth here: there is no such thing as natural-born Giant Killers. No one is born with courage. Courage doesn't work that way.

In the book *Win the Day* (the best book Jon read in 2021),

author Mark Batterson retells the story of former baseball player George "The Shotgun" Shuba. George's swing was once described as "natural as a smile." What people didn't know was that Shuba developed his swing by practicing it time and time again. This is why Shuba smirked when he heard this sentiment.

Shuba then responded, *"You call this natural? I swung a forty-four-ounce bat six hundred times a night, 4,200 times a week, 47,200 swings every winter . . . in my humble opinion, there are no naturals."*

There are those who develop courage and those who do not. This section is all about getting our swings in.

STRATEGY #1: RECALL PAST VICTORIES

Courage is not a self-generated virtue, it's a derivative virtue, meaning courage is not something you impose as much as it is something you import.

David's courage was imported from two places: his God and his past. Do you remember how back in driver's education classes they instructed students to use the rearview mirror every three to five seconds? Their point was clear, in order to move forward you had to know what was behind you. The same is true in releasing courage.

David moved forward because he consistently looked back to see and remember the faithfulness of God during fear. For David, the victories over the bear and lion were no longer victories of chance, they developed into a Stone of Courage. In this moment, David's past was doing something for his present.

David said, *"The Lord who rescued me from the paw of the lion and the paw of the bear will rescue me from the hand of this Philistine"* (1 Samuel 17:37 (NIV)).

David remembered that. The question is, have you forgotten?

There are times we need to delete the past and there are other times we must draw from our past. This is one of those times. The courage you need for this moment will be imported from your past.

Recall that day you gave birth.

Recall that day you crossed the finish line.

Recall that day you chose to have that crucial conversation.

Recall that evening you remained sober for *one more day*.

If you did it then, you can do it now. If God was with you in that, He'll be with you in this. Recalling past victories is a strategy that activates courage. This is why we recommend that you chronicle your victories in a journal or in a notes app. Doing so will allow you to recall your victories and look back through your past entries as often as needed, and recall your victories over lions and bears. As we look back on moments of triumph, courage comes forth and is strengthened. It's powerful and it helps us practice the strategy of remembering.

STRATEGY #2: DIP YOUR TOE IN

Sometimes, before we're ready to toe the line against a giant, we first need to dip our toe in the water. We need to find small opportunities to step into the very thing we're afraid of. Exposing ourselves to the very things that scare us will perhaps reveal that we allowed the fear to grow bigger than it needed to be in the first place.

One of the most popular fears among people is the fear of public speaking. Jerry Seinfeld once said, "*According to most studies, people's number one fear is public speaking. Number two is death. Death is number two. Does that sound right? This means to the average person, if you go to a funeral, you're better off in the casket than doing the eulogy.*"

Throwing someone with this fear up on stage, in front of thousands of people, will likely not go well for that person (or their underwear). Instead, it's best if they find small opportunities to stand before a small group of people and speak for short periods of time. After some experiences under their belt, the crowd size can grow, the talks can get longer, and the fear diminishes. Remember, before David killed a nine-footer, he killed a bear and lion.

If you suffer from fear of rejection, you don't need acceptance to overcome your fear, you need more rejection (again, small doses). Yes, it sounds harsh, but we need more exposure to the things that we're unsure of, or that terrify us, in order to develop the confidence to overcome them. We learned this at the allergy doctor: if you have an allergy, what is the best path forward? Small doses of the very thing you're allergic to.

Afraid of roller coasters? Start on small coasters and repeat as much as necessary.

Afraid to talk to the cutie at the gym? Start by just saying hello once.

Afraid to speak up in class? Start raising your hand once a day.

Afraid to start the company you've always dreamed of? Determine one small step you could take to move you forward without fully committing.

In what ways could you start dipping your toe in the water for some mild exposure to that big fear that prevents you from living in confidence?

STRATEGY #3: START WITH THE END IN MIND

I (Blake) told the story in a previous book of how I was once bullied in college. You may have had one in middle school, or high school (I did too), but I was lucky enough to have a bully in college as well, during my senior year no less!

I had dated and parted ways with a great girl months before she began dating my soon-to-be bully. He obviously saw me as a threat to their new relationship and confronted me one day in the cafeteria. In a not-so-nice tone, he essentially told me to, "Stay away from her, or else!"

Now I must admit, he scared me. He was a pitcher on the baseball team and was much larger than I was at the time. He also had a reputation as a fighter (like Goliath did). He could easily "bruise my neck meat." I immediately felt the need to stay away from this ex-girlfriend, even though we had remained friends after our breakup. And when I say "friends," it was pretty much just exchanging pleasantries when we'd see each other on campus. We both had moved on.

Well, as luck would have it, that very evening in the

cafeteria, this ex-girlfriend came up to me and joined me at the table where I was eating. I quickly looked over my shoulder to see if I was about to get jumped from behind. I found myself being very short and rude to her so she would leave and not get me in any trouble with her boyfriend. She did indeed leave. She was very disappointed with my behavior and so was I. I felt horrible afterward. She had done nothing to warrant me to treat her so rudely. I knew I couldn't let this continue. It wasn't fair to me, and it wasn't fair to her. I knew I needed to stand up to my bully. I couldn't let this be the end of the story.

With a mouth as dry as cotton, I confronted my bully in his dorm room that night. I let him know that I was not a threat to his relationship but that it also wasn't fair for me to feel like I couldn't be nice to her when we crossed paths—she deserved better than that. He agreed, we shook hands, and I left his room feeling much taller than I did when I walked in.

Can you see past your Giant of Fear to what could exist on the other side? Might there be something (new ground) on the other side of that giant that simply must happen—something that you just can't let go undone? What end goal might drive you to overcome the Giant of Fear?

- Could your end goal of defending the poor help you overcome your fear of speaking up?
- Could your end goal of financial freedom drive you to overcome your fear of starting that new business or finishing that degree?
- Could your end goal of raising courageous children help you overcome the pervasiveness of fear-based parenting?

- Could your end goal of getting married help you overcome that fear of asking her out?
- Could your end goal of living a healthy life help you overcome that bag of Doritos you're crushing right now? (Just sayin'.)
- Could your end goal of experiencing God's best for your life help you overcome the fear of ending that relationship?

We think you get the point. As you know, you'll never steal second with your foot on first. Courage is not a gift you're born with, it's a skill you develop. There are no naturals!

THE GIANT OF COMFORT

You are in danger of living a life so comfortable and soft, that you will die without ever realizing your true potential.

—David Goggins

DISCERN COMFORT (S2)

COMFORT IS YOUR enemy, not your ally.

Of all the giants outlined in this book, you better keep your eye on this one. He's subtle and he's deceitful. He's the king of the head fake. His goal is to dull your edge. His mission is to render your life half lived.

The Giant of Comfort lures you with gluttony but drowns you with mediocrity.

Here's the problem, I (Jon) like to be comfortable, I really do. I like my sweatpants, my seat warmers, my slippers, and my comfort food. For me, it's deep-dish pizza and Sour Patch Kids. Add to that seventy-five-degree weather, a slight breeze, and college football and you can call it a day.

According to a couple of sources, the term "comfort zone" originated in reference to the temperature zone of sixty-seven to seventy-eight degrees where we're most comfortable and feel neither hot nor cold. When I read that I immediately thought, "This is the climate I hope exists in Eternity." Sixty-seven to seventy-eight degrees every day sounds amazing, but let's think about that for a second.

Think about all that happens on either side of that comfort zone. If you have that comfort zone, you can forget about sledding or skiing. There are no snowball fights or ice skating. Cancel your snowmobile trips and sell your ice fishing gear. And think of all you'd miss on the other side of that comfort zone. If it only gets up to seventy-eight degrees, there will be far fewer sandcastles and far fewer beach trips. The lakes in Wisconsin or Michigan won't get warm enough to water ski or wake surf, and those of you who love to tan, you can forget about getting golden brown each summer.

Don't misunderstand me, some comfort is good, but often, **comfort becomes our kryptonite**.

Do you remember what kryptonite did to Superman? When exposed to this fictional material, Superman was just a man—no super, just man. The extraordinary became ordinary. The uncommon was common. Ol' Clark would slowly become weakened when proximate to kryptonite.

Comfort is your kryptonite. Overexposure to comfort has pickpocketed the potential of humans since the beginning of time. We must see comfort for what it is and what it is not. Comfort is like California—it's a nice place to visit but we don't recommend living there.

COMFORT COSTS

Comfort comes easy, but it doesn't come cheap. In fact, it can be quite costly (like living in California). We typically do the math, but only on one side of the equation. We add up what it will cost our body if we sign up to run a marathon—the time to train, the cost of new shoes, etc.—but we almost never do the cost of living with that bucket-list item going unchecked.

The Giant of Comfort is sneaky and dangerous. It's a wolf in sheep's clothing. This giant works its way into our lives and appears to be much more of a friend than an adversary. Again, comfort is your enemy, not your ally.

The low-hanging fruit to consider here, as we look around our world, is the fact that comfort costs many people their health. One in every three Americans is obese. That equates to a lot of "comfort food" being enjoyed way too often by way too many. Using food for comfort is a real struggle for many. That, coupled with the comfort of the couch, is costing many individuals their health and quality of life.

Comfort might also cost us significantly at work. Maybe we've settled into that comfortable role that no longer challenges us but pays the bills. The comfort we find in the job might be preventing us from striving for something that brings us even greater happiness and has a greater positive impact on this world.

Comfort may cost us in our marriages. We've been with our significant other for years. The honeymoon phase ended a long time ago. We're too comfortable with them. We stop pursuing them as we should. We're existing, not thriving. Perhaps we're so comfortable, we let our guard down and don't protect our marriage vows the way we should.

Ultimately, comfort costs us joy—the joy of a deeper and healthier life, the joy of a more fulfilling career, the joy of a great marriage, the joy of a wonderfully uncommon existence in this life. How much longer will we allow the Giant of Comfort to rob us of the uncommon life we are meant to have?

In our battles to defeat the Giant of Comfort, our brains can work against us. One of the brain's primary functions is to seek comfort for us. The brain wants to keep us in our comfort zones, and we're sure you've experienced it. We hear the message from our brain every time we begin to push our bodies in that tough workout—you know, the message that says, "stop," "slow down," "you can't keep up this pace," or "ease up." That's your brain talking. The brain wants to keep your body in a comfortable state.

Great athletes have learned to ignore these messages from the brain. They've been able to push their bodies past their comfort zones time and time again. They hear the same brain messages that we average Joes and Janes hear, but they've chosen not to listen to them.

I (Jon) know the Giant of Comfort like I know my name. In many ways, this has been my life's greatest battle. From pulling up short to avoiding hard things, comfort and I know one another all too well. I've experienced this in many situations—swimming is one of them. Ever since I was a small boy, as soon as I got into a swimming pool, my brain told me to get out, as soon as possible! My chest would tighten, and an overwhelming feeling would set in as I feverishly scurried for the ladder to escape. Comfort for me was watching others swim while I sat poolside, and yet, there's been a nagging curiosity all these years about what would happen if I truly faced this giant.

For whatever reason, 2020 became that year. I became enamored with the idea of becoming a triathlete. Was it a mid-life crisis or a mid-life opportunity? I chose to believe the latter. To start and finish an Olympic distance triathlon filled my heart and mind. I imagined what it would feel like to have that medal around my neck. I also imagined how embarrassed my daughters and wife would be when they saw me in a skin-tight tri-suit, so I **got in the water**.

My first time at the lap pool was a disaster. In fact, the first three months of *getting in the water*, three days a week, were a disaster. I swam in discomfort. My lungs were on fire. My arms were tired. But the real issue was not my body, it was my brain. I cannot put into words how afraid I was of drowning. This would be my experience until December 23, 2020. That day is a day I will never forget.

It clicked. I swam one hundred yards without stopping! My eyes were as big as saucers—I could not believe it. In that moment, I experienced something far more enjoyable than comfort; I experienced the sheer delight of defeating a life-long giant.

Six months later, in three hours and forty-six minutes, I completed my first Olympic triathlon. Due to the heat and hills, my time was not impressive, but man, did I feel good when they put that medal around my neck. I was a triath-lete! I am a triathlete! I am now training for an Ironman70.3 race.

I embraced and continue to embrace the process of becoming comfortable with being uncomfortable.

DISCOVER DISCIPLINE (S3)

HERE, OUR FIVE-STEP Process for Killing Giants moves from discerning to discovery. We've become clear of the obstacle, now we must identify the strategy. This is what Step 3 (S3) is all about. **If the giant is comfort, the strategy is discipline.**

> *Discipline is doing what you really don't want to do so you can do what you really want to do.*
>
> —Jeff Fisher

Discipline can be defined this way: the time and effort it takes to develop firm control of one's daily decisions.

The Giant of Comfort wants to be in control of our decisions, and when he controls our decisions, he controls us. Unlike other strategies we detail in this book, discipline is not one we have to seek out. This "stone" is often laying on the ground right next to us, maybe even calling out to us, "Choose me! Choose me!" Finding it is not the issue; choosing it, daily—now that's a different story. Choosing discipline is often what separates amateurs from professionals. Amateurs back away at the onset of the pain of discipline. Professionals, on the other hand, embrace the pain because they know it's doing something *for* them.

This reminds me of a story from Joshua Medcalf's book *Chop Wood, Carry Water*:

> *There once was a Japanese man named Kota who designed and built homes for thirty years and became a true master of his craft. It wasn't talent that made him great but his passion and grit. He was always the first in and last out at work, and no matter the obstacle, he always treated every home as if it was his own and poured his heart and soul into everything he built.*
>
> *After thirty years, he told his boss that he was retiring. But his boss told him their company had just received a contract to build a home for a very important client and they really wanted him to be the one to build it. Kota was frustrated, but after talking with his wife, he reluctantly agreed to build this one last house. However, he made it very clear this was the last one.*
>
> *And the difference with this one was obvious: his heart simply wasn't in it. He phoned it in. He showed up late and left early and didn't put in the care and attention to detail that he normally did. He knew it would be up to code, but he also knew it was far from his best work. He had built homes twenty years ago that were much better. But sure enough, it passed inspection. And in the final project meeting, his boss told him, "Thank you, Kota! We just have one more thing!"*

Kota began to get upset because he thought they were going to ask him to build another house. But instead, his boss gave him a small box with a red ribbon and said, "We are so grateful for you. Your years of mastery have made our company great. This gift is just a small token of our appreciation."

Kota opened the box and discovered a set of shiny new keys.

His boss smiled, "The house is yours! You deserve it!"

*Kota's heart sank. Unbeknownst to him, the whole time he had been building **his own house**.*

Friends, you are building your own house. Every act of discipline is constructing a life that blesses you and those you love most. Is it painful? Of course, but it's less painful than the pain of regret.

It's been said before, *"Choose your pain—the pain of discipline or the pain of regret."*

Again, if the giant is comfort, the strategy is discipline. Here's the good news: if you follow Christ, this strategy of self-discipline already resides within you, in and through the Holy Spirit. Discovering this truth is a game-changer.

The Bible says, *"For the Spirit God gave us does not make us timid, but gives us power, love and **self-discipline**"* (2 Timothy 1:7 (NIV)).

Like other virtues, self-discipline is more God-initiated than self-generated. Simply put: our job is to abide, His job is to provide. This is why we often say to take a closer look at the story and you will see how David is not the hero, God is.

David said to the Philistine, "You come against me with sword and spear and javelin, but I come against you in the name of the LORD Almighty."

—1 Samuel 17:45(NIV)

This is where we part ways with other self-help books. We're not against them or the authors who wrote them, it's just that we are *really* for God and the invitation He extends to every one of us. His way is better. Intrinsic self-discipline instead of extrinsic self-discipline is a better strategy. God's plan relies on God's power. Again, your job is to abide, God's job is to provide. And as you abide, you will experience God deposit self-discipline into your life and through your life.

DISCIPLINE DEPOSITS

Comfort costs, but discipline deposits. Each time we choose discipline, a small deposit is made toward becoming that better version of ourselves. We may not see the results of the deposit initially, but it's there. The results from discipline are kind of like believing in God. We don't always see or feel God, but that doesn't mean He's not there or that He's not working. We don't always see or feel the results of our discipline, but we have to trust that it's working.

Oftentimes, in order to see the deposit we made today by choosing discipline, we must first make the same deposit consistently over a long period of time. And that's what makes choosing a disciplined lifestyle so difficult; it may not often catapult us to where we want to be right away. It's a slow play.

Many of us see it at the start of every year. The gyms are filled with those committed to finally getting in better shape (many of them made the same commitment in previous years as well). They start out showing great consistency for a few weeks or maybe a couple of months, but they grow impatient because they're not seeing the dramatic results they'd hoped to see. They've perhaps been sedentary for years and they expect that a couple of months in a gym will undo all the effects of the lifestyle they've had for years. So many of these individuals get frustrated and quit. They abandon the small deposits they've made up to that point.

Choosing to be disciplined in one area of life can often lead to us being more disciplined in other areas. This is why discipline is a keystone skill. It cascades into other things. For example, as we make the choice to be disciplined in our exercise habits, we often choose to be more disciplined in our eating habits. Or maybe it becomes easier to choose the discipline of getting up early to exercise so our busy schedules don't get in the way of establishing a healthier lifestyle.

Choosing discipline is like compounding our deposits, which means we'll see results faster.

Imagine the dedicated employee who, over a long period of time, has been a disciplined employee. They've consistently arrived to work on time while others have not. They've chosen to learn and grow in their role while others have chosen to do the bare minimum. They've chosen to be kind to their coworkers even when it's hard to be. They've chosen to show respect to their customers even when their customers disrespect them. Eventually, all these deposits will reveal themselves. It might be a pay raise, a promotion, a better opportunity at another company, greater influence with others, or all of these. Long-term, consistent deposits made through choosing discipline always provide a reward.

This is the promise of Hebrews 12:11 (NIV): *"No discipline is enjoyable while it is happening—it's painful! But afterward, there will be a peaceful harvest of right living for those who are trained in this way."*

DEVELOP DISCIPLINE (S4)

IN THIS SECTION we'll highlight three strategies that will develop your discipline. Over time, Giant Killers habituate self-discipline through ongoing practice. It's time to make our thousand putts. Alan Iverson does not like S4. *"Practice!"*

James Clear was transparent: *"Winners and losers have the same goals . . . Ultimately, it is your commitment to the process that will determine your progress."* As we practice discipline, we alchemize pain into a lifelong ally.

These are three strategies for developing discipline that aid in the process of alchemy:

STRATEGY #1: AIM SMALL, MISS SMALL

There was a scene in the movie *The Patriot*, when Mel Gibson asks his sons, *"Boys, do you remember what I told you about shooting?"* Their answer: *"Aim small, miss small."*

Often, we experience the defeat of missing big. Why? Because you're aiming big. Too big. United States Navy Admiral William H. McRaven once famously said, "*If you want to change the world, start off by making your bed.*"

Aim small!

Some have wanted to become readers. They subscribe to the maxim that "readers are leaders." We agree. But a year ends and a year begins and still the stack of unread books increases, as does your feeling of defeat. You said, "This year I am going to read fifty-two books." The result? A big miss.

What if instead, you aimed small by reading for two minutes a day.

I (Jon) bought a Kindle this year and I leave it on my bedside table. Instead of scrolling through Facebook (I intentionally leave my phone downstairs), I pick up my Kindle and read for two minutes.

Aim small, miss small!

If you want to swim 1,700 yards without stopping (Olympic-distance tri), start by committing to swim the distance of the pool. Aim small.

If you want to live a life filled with years of sobriety, start with today. It's true, "A journey of a thousand miles begins with a single step."

When we aim big, we put ourselves in a position that requires tremendous willpower. Every now and again we'll hit the mark, but not consistently.

In his book, *Atomic Habits*, James Clear explains it this way: "*When scientists analyze people who appear to have tremendous self-control, it turns out those individuals aren't all that different from those who are struggling. Instead, 'disciplined' people are better at structuring their lives in a way that does not require heroic willpower and self-control. In other words, they spend less time in tempting situations."*

Back away from the three-point line and move into the paint. Give yourself layup opportunities that will build momentum to fuel even greater discipline in your life. Aim small!

STRATEGY #2: PUT YOUR FEELINGS IN THE BACK SEAT

Living with discipline is difficult. There's a 100 percent guarantee that you will not always *feel* like choosing to practice discipline. There will be many days when you don't feel like getting up early, when you don't feel like going to the gym, don't feel like skipping dessert, don't feel like loving your spouse, don't feel like being positive, don't feel like putting in great effort at work, and countless other situations. These feelings are to be noticed but not trusted. We agree wholeheartedly with Jesus who said, *"The spirit is willing but the flesh is weak"* (Matthew 46:21 (NIV)).

Feelings are like small children. They have an important place in the vehicle, but that place is in the back seat. We're not stoics; emotions are part of how God made you. Your emotions matter and they must be noticed. Notice them, feel them, and then place them where they belong. We've got to stop living a life so strongly guided by feelings and choose to live by principles (or standards) instead.

In order to live by principles, we must first have principles we choose to live by (you choose them, nobody else). We know that not all of you have those established, so we certainly encourage you to spend some time establishing some (or if you do have them, spend time determining if they need to change based on your current season of life). Principles can greatly improve the quality of life, both for you and those you care about.

To create sound principles, it helps to have an idea of our desired direction in life as well as a good understanding of what things are important to us.

Here are some examples of principles some may choose to live by. These are only examples. Yours should be personal to you.

- Positive—I choose to be positive in all situations because life is happening for me.
- Fit—I pursue fitness in body, finances, and relationships.
- Kind—I am kind to everyone, regardless.
- Inclusive—I treat everyone with an equal amount of respect.
- Generous—I live and give from an abundance mindset.
- Selfless—I put the needs of others before my own.
- Hardworking—I strive to work hard in all things I commit myself to FILO (which stands for first in, last out).
- Servant Leader—I choose to use my influence to serve those I lead.
- Loyal—My friends and family will never doubt my devotion.
- Faithful Spouse—I choose to be ever-faithful to my spouse.

When establishing principles, a good question to ask our-selves is, "What do I want to be known for?" Or perhaps we might consider what we'd like others to say about us at our funeral.

Hand your principles the keys. It's time to let them drive.

STRATEGY #3: EAT THE BIGGER FROG FIRST

Mark Twain once said, *"If it's your job to eat a frog, it's best to do it first thing in the morning. And If it's your job to eat two frogs, it's best to eat the biggest one first."* This is both hilarious and incredibly helpful. Discipline often includes prioritiz-ing what we will give our time and energy to. The easiest things shout for our attention, and the hardest things re-main silent.

The bigger frog, for many of us, is pushing our bodies phys-ically through working out. If that's you, may we suggest working out first thing in the morning? That's the bigger frog. For others, it's prayer or planning out your day. It doesn't matter what your bigger frog is; what matters is that you eat it as early as possible.

I've heard it said that it is wise to organize your day so that by noon, you've already had a successful day. What great advice that is. Those who discipline themselves eat the big-ger frog first.

Ask yourself which to-do item seems larger than any other items on your to-do list. Resist comfort, activate discipline, and make yo' self a big ol' frog sandwich.

How we begin our day sets the tone for the rest of it. This is why we *win the morning* with discipline. It's also why I (Jon) tackle my writing responsibilities before ten a.m. For me, writing is a dadgum *frog*, a big one at that. I've got miles to go to become great at "big frog eating" but I'm committed to developing that skill.

Resist comfort, activate discipline.

Build your house. Eat the bigger frog first.

Amateur hour is over. Welcome to the big leagues!

THE GIANT OF SELF-DOUBT

Our doubts are traitors, and make us lose the good we might oft win, by fearing to attempt.

—William Shakespeare

DISCERN SELF-DOUBT (S2)

SHAKESPEARE WAS RIGHT. Self-doubt is a Benedict Arnold we must discern accurately. This giant is formed from our experiences and our interactions with others as we grow. Perhaps it's formed when our family splits up, when we fail the test, when we miss the game-winning shot, when we're teased by our classmates, the way our parents spoke to us, when they dumped us, or thousands of other instances we won't take time to list.

These experiences may very well cause that voice in our head to grow into the Giant of Self-Doubt. We're confident you know the voice we're talking about—the one that might tell you:

- "You're horrible."
- "There's no way you can do that."
- "You're not good enough."
- "You don't deserve that."

Plain and simple, self-doubt is a mental habit that forms and causes us to question our worth. Now, a certain amount of self-doubt can be good for us and protect us from being overly confident and making poor decisions (i.e., a five-foot, four-inch person who believes they can play the position of center on a professional basketball team might waste far too much time chasing an impossible dream). But self-doubt can certainly grow to be a giant we face regularly.

Here are some ways you can tell if your self-doubt has become a giant:

- Self-doubt cripples your ability to make everyday decisions.
- Self-doubt is often your first reaction in many areas of life.
- Self-doubt causes you to regret your decisions.
- Self-doubt prevents you from focusing on the task at hand.
- Self-doubt contradicts what everyone says about you.
- You have a hard time taking compliments or giving yourself any credit.
- You often feel like you're not enough.
- You often seek reassurance from others.
- You are surrounded by others who feed your self-doubt.

Therapist Nick Wignall shared in an article that self-doubt tends to take three primary forms:

1. Imposter syndrome: A fear of being discovered to be a fraud, that you don't deserve anything you achieve. (Example: You might be great at your job, but you don't think you're nearly as good as those around you, and one day you'll make a mistake that will reveal that to everyone.)
2. Self-sabotage: A tendency to undermine your goals, values, and desires. (Example: Your diet has been

going great for weeks, but you go off the rails and binge on junk food for a few days. You likely think you don't deserve the positive results a healthy diet could provide.)

3. Indecisiveness: You struggle with making even the smallest of decisions because of the possible consequences you'll face if you make a bad decision. (Example: It's your birthday and your coworkers want you to pick where you'd like to go to lunch, but you defer to others because you're afraid someone might not like your choice.)

The Giant of Self-Doubt has been my (Blake) nemesis since the split of my family when I was a toddler. My giant stands across the battlefield from me and continually yells, "You're not enough!" Early in life, it didn't really matter the circumstance, I just wasn't enough in my mind. I wasn't strong enough, smart enough, tall enough, brave enough, funny enough, tough enough, capable enough, etc.

Not fully understanding the situation because of my age, I felt like my mom and dad gave me away—that they didn't want me, that they rejected me. I didn't know my dad was spending a lot of time behind bars and thus wasn't able to be a good parent to me. I didn't know of the difficulties my mom was facing trying to raise four young kids on her own with little income. I just felt that they chose *not* to be with me. Therefore, there must be something lacking in me that made them not want me to live with them anymore (again, what the voice in my head told me, and I listened).

One of the early symptoms of my self-doubt was my desire to be someone else. Because I didn't think that being Blake was enough, I tried to be the type of person that I thought others would like. And that version of me could change depending on the crowd I was in. I was like a chameleon, ever-changing to try to fit in and match my environment. It was like I owned these different masks I would put on in certain situations to hide the real me and pretend to be a version of me that others would think was "enough."

I've worn the mask of the funny guy, the tough guy, the sensitive guy, the jock, the smart guy, and the spiritual guy. The thing I learned from wearing these masks was that, eventually, people see through them. Choosing not to be me, and choosing these masks instead, was doing more damage than good to my identity and my integrity as a person. I couldn't see it then, but I would have been much better served just being me.

Battles against the Giant of Self-Doubt have caused deep wounds that have been slow to heal. This giant has won countless victories over me. Some of its more memorable victories over me include:

- not excelling more in school.
- failing to be a better friend.
- refusing to join sports teams.
- quitting a football team on the second day of practice.
- not attending my dream college.
- turning down a great opportunity to go to grad school.
- passing on a great job offer in a different city.
- delaying the pursuit of my dreams.

This giant stifles the stewardship of our one and only life, and robs us of living our best life, which is why we believe the wealthiest places on Earth are found in our local cemeteries.

Think about it. Cemeteries are rich with:

- dreams never pursued.
- inventions never created.
- love unshared.
- hopes never fulfilled.
- million-dollar ideas ignored.
- best-selling books unwritten.
- help never offered.
- potential unreached.
- wisdom never passed down.
- memories never made.
- beauty unrealized.

So why should you toe the line against the Giant of Self-Doubt? We think the answer is simple: **because you were made for more.**

DISCOVER CONFIDENCE (S3)

Faith is a living, daring confidence in God's grace, so sure and certain that a man could stake his life on it a thousand times.

—Martin Luther

IT'S TIME WE discover a "daring confidence."

If we're going to fight the Giant of Self-Doubt, we need a Stone of Confidence. Confidence helps give us the belief and the courage to advance. Confidence causes us to show up despite self-doubt, even if we think the outcome might not end up in our favor. It helps us throw our hat in the ring and try.

What David lacked in size, he made up for in confidence. In 1 Samuel 17:32 (NIV), David says to King Saul, *"Let no one lose heart on account of this Philistine; your servant will go and fight him."* It was like the freshman on the varsity football team going up to his coach with the game on the line and saying, "Put me in, Coach!"

Instead of shrinking back, David surged forward with a daring confidence that comes from God. In verse 37 (NIV) David says, *"The Lord who rescued me from the paw of the lion and the paw of the bear will rescue me from the hand of this Philistine."*

Instead of focusing on his ability alone, David focused on God's power. If God did it then, He'll do it now. It begs the question, where is your confidence coming from? David possessed confidence, yes, but his confidence came from God. This is why everyone else retreated while David—and David alone—advanced.

The amount of confidence we need is going to be in proportion to the size of the giant we need to face. The bigger the giant, the more confidence we need.

Here are some examples of how confidence might be used.

EXAMPLE 1

Self-doubt: "There's a volunteer role at church I think I'd enjoy doing but I doubt anyone would consider me. I likely don't have the personality they need for that role."

Confidence could be: "I'll talk privately to someone on staff to tell them I'm interested if they need help."

There's likely not a ton of confidence required here because it's not a paid position and you don't even have to tell anyone else that you expressed interest. So if you're not selected, no one will know but you. The Giant of Self-Doubt is certainly present but he's not fully grown.

EXAMPLE 2

Self-doubt: "A position opened up at work that I'd like to apply for. I applied for a similar position two years ago and got passed over. There will be so many quality applicants that I likely won't get it."

Confidence could be: "I'll email my supervisor to inform them that I'll be applying for the open position."

This example requires sizable confidence for several reasons: (1) You've already failed to get this position once before, (2) your coworkers will know you've applied (and failed again if you don't get it), and (3) you'll be competing with many others for the job. The Giant of Self-Doubt has grown into a very sizable opponent.

EXAMPLE 3

Self-doubt: "My boss has approached me about assuming a new position with the company in a neighboring state where I'd be managing others for the first time. I'm inclined to turn it down since I have no experience managing others, I don't know anyone in that part of the country, and I'm afraid I'd fail and make my boss look bad for selecting me."

Confidence could be: "This new position really stretches me, but after weighing the pros and cons, it's a great opportunity for me. I have to accept this job!"

This final example requires a whole heap of confidence. Confidence in this example needs to be the size of a boulder because the Giant of Self-Doubt is ginormous! Many opportunities in life will stretch us, making us uncomfortable and thus causing self-doubt to bubble to the surface. Managing for the first time, plus moving away from your comfort zone to a place where you know no one and having that fear of failure, adds up to one really big giant! But your boss has obviously chosen you for a reason. They have confidence in your abilities to be successful in this role, or else they wouldn't have approached you in the first place. Maybe you need to have that same confidence in yourself.

Discovering the Stone of Confidence (S3) can be life changing. It can help release chains that might have held us captive for years. Self-doubt almost always focuses on what you don't have, while confidence focuses on what you do have. The Giant of Self-Doubt is a professional at exposing all that *isn't* in your inventory. Confidence flips the script and says, *You're right. I may not have a javelin and spear, but I do have a sling and stones.*

Several years ago, I (Jon) heard a sermon by Louie Giglio titled "Take the Step" that impacted me greatly. Louie and his wife, Shelly, lead an amazing movement called The Passion Conference, as well as Passion City Church in the suburbs of Atlanta. Louie has had a tremendous impact on young leaders around the world and I am one of them.

In his talk, Louie spoke of the time he managed to take the most difficult steps of his life. These steps involved scaling one of the highest mountains in Europe, known as the Matterhorn. Each step was met with a lack of oxygen and an abundance of self-doubt.

I walked away thinking two things after listening to Louie:

1. Self-doubt grows as we focus on the summit instead of the next step.
2. Self-doubt grows as we agree with lies instead of the truth.

Let me explain both.

When we focus or fixate on the summit, on the victory, on the business making it, on the book being fully written, or on the kids being fully raised, we are quickly met with a pile of unanswered questions. As those unanswered questions pile up, so does self-doubt. We stand frozen in the reality that we have no idea how we will make it to the top. There are times when focusing on the end helps and there are times when it doesn't.

The Israelite Army fixated on the "how"; David focused on the "now." David took the step. As I look back over the last ten years of providing leadership to Mission Church, I had no idea of how we would get to where we are today. The view at year ten is stunning. To stand here today and see all that God has done is a vista I could only imagine ten years ago. How it would be accomplished, I had no idea, but praise Jesus, a handful of friends and I decided to take the step.

Here's what we're saying: stop focusing on the summit and start focusing on your next step.

That non-profit you've dreamed of starting, take the step.

That relationship you've longed to restore, take the step.

That race you've longed to complete, take the step.

That twelve-step program you've imagined finishing, take the step.

That neighbor you've considered befriending, take the step.

Take the step!

And once you've taken that step, take the next one after that. The truism holds up: *"A journey of a million miles begins with a **single step**."*

Secondly, self-doubt is fertilized by lies. Your enemy, according to the Bible, is known as Satan. His objective is to "steal, kill, and destroy" every good thing—and God thing—going on in your life. This we most likely don't need to convince you of, but let's be clear: if God called you to advance, Satan wants you to retreat.

In the gospel of John, Jesus refers to Satan as the "Father of Lies," for all he can do is lie. When it comes to self-doubt, he often whispers in our ear, "You can't."

This is where Louie comes in. Louie shared with us his response when that lie begins to thunder in our hearts and minds. Instead of blowing up or quickly defending, beat Satan at his own game. The response is this: "I can't, but God can."

Jon can't, but God can.

Blake can't, but God can.

Add your name in. Try it. Feel pressure dissipate. Feel power rise.

One of the most important truths in Scripture is this: *"You, dear children, are from God and have overcome them, because the one who is **in you** is **greater** than the one who is in the world"* (1 John 4:4 (NIV)).

Christ in me is the stone that defeats the Giant of Self-Doubt.

This is where *Christian Confidence* comes from. It comes from *"Christ in you, the hope of glory."* My confidence comes from who Christ is and who He says I am. This is not a confidence in my flesh, this is a confidence in the One who resides within me. I can't, but God can.

We promise you, this shift in mindset can change your life. It has ours.

Agree with truth. Take the step.

DEVELOP CONFIDENCE (S4)

JUST AS DAVID intentionally searched for specific stones he would take into battle, we need to intentionally do the same. This takes repetition, or what we call *mental memory*, which comes through intentional practice. Remember, there are "no naturals," which is why *developing* (S4) confidence is so key. It's time to do the work. It's time to cultivate confidence one day at a time. This requires a lot of work over a long period of time for many of us to see an improvement, but make no mistake, confidence is a skill that can be developed, regardless of your current proficiency level.

Here are seven strategies to help you develop confidence.

STRATEGY #1: EMBRACE YOUR SELF-DOUBT

Sounds crazy, right? Embracing the thing we're trying to overcome. But psychologist Nick Wignall describes the mental health notion, *"What we resist, persists,"* meaning if we treat something like a threat, then the brain will treat it like a threat.

Wignall goes on to say, *"So, if you get in the habit of imme-diately trying to run away from self-doubt (say, by distracting yourself from it) or trying to eliminate it (arguing with yourself about why it's dumb to feel that way), the self-doubt will only come back stronger the next time.*

The antidote is to briefly acknowledge your self-doubt and let it know that, while you don't like it, you're not afraid of it. Literally talk to your own self-doubt and say this:

Hey there, Self-Doubt. You're not my favorite but I get that you're only trying to help. Go ahead and hang out if you like, but I'm getting back to [whatever it is you want to be doing].

In other words, to embrace your self-doubt means to acknowledge it and be willing to have it, and then refocus your energy and attention on getting on with life.

Do this consistently and you will slowly train your brain to not be so reactive to its own self-doubt. And that will make it far easier for you to move past it."

STRATEGY #2: CONFIDENCE SPILLS OVER

So maybe you lack confidence in multiple areas of life—not only do you lack confidence in regard to your fitness level but also in your ability to make good presentations at work, to be a good parent, or to lead your team or department with excellence. The good news is that if you work to build confidence in one area, it often spills over into other areas (killing a bear and a lion apparently spills over to killing gi-ants, by the way). It's like the pyramid of cups where water fills the cup at the top of the pyramid, and it overflows once full, spilling water into the cups below.

It's common to see someone that is unhappy with their appearance lacking in confidence. But if they put in the work necessary to improve the way they view themselves outwardly, their confidence will improve. And if they can feel more confident about their appearance, that confidence will spill over into other areas of their life, such as their confidence in social settings or their confidence at work.

Some of us may be confident about our abilities in a particular area of life. Perhaps you can focus on becoming even more confident in that area so that the confidence you have in there can spill over into other areas.

Regardless of how confident you may be in a particular area of life, the more you apply practice to an area, the more confident you will become in that area. Find ways to practice. If you're not confident in your public speaking ability, practice public speaking. If you're not confident in your body, put in the necessary practice to either change your body in a way that gives you confidence or put in the mental practice to change your way of thinking so you learn to be confident in the body you have.

With consistent, intentional practice applied to anything, you will improve. There's a reason why athletes practice the skills they need for their sport over and over. That's called muscle memory. With practice, you improve. As you improve, you gain confidence. With confidence, you can defeat the Giant of Self-Doubt.

STRATEGY #3: FIND YOUR "WHY"

We all have a reason for doing the things we do—we refer

to this as our "why." Simon Sinek made this notion famous a few years ago in his book *Start with Why*. We believe to our core, if you lose your why, you will lose your way. Our why drives us to make the commitments we make and determines the amount of time and effort we devote to those commitments.

The size of your why will determine the size of your work.

You'll see a much different level of effort from a teammate who's on the team only due to their parents' demands versus the one who absolutely loves the sport they play.

Self-doubt wants us to forget about our why. It will cloud our vision and try to prevent us from seeing a compelling reason to take action. If we let it, self-doubt will prevent us from making a commitment ("I won't join the team because I doubt I can add value.") or reduce our effort in our existing commitments ("I don't think I can be as successful as others at my job, so I won't try to be."). How might self-doubt be affecting your commitments?

Having a strong why can give us the confidence to help us overcome our self-doubt and pursue our dreams and do amazing things. A strong why can motivate us to try in spite of our self-doubt or even the doubt others may have about us.

A strong why can help:

- A high school athlete receive an athletic scholarship and become the first in their family to attend college.

- The stuttering kid become a TV host (i.e., Steve Harvey).
- A deaf and blind girl become an author and disability rights activist (i.e., Helen Keller).
- A girl survive abuse, neglect, and sex trafficking to earn a law degree and PhD (i.e., Dr. Katrina Rosenblatt).

STRATEGY #4: SPEND TIME WITH THE RIGHT PEOPLE

Deep down you know who they are—the ones who aren't much good for you. Perhaps they've been a friend for a long time. Perhaps they're a family member. But despite how close you may be to them, they rob you of confidence. They say and do things that make you question your worth.

If you wanted to become a marine biologist, it would make sense that, during the course of your studies, you'd spend time with those who are already marine biologists. At the very least you'd spend a lot of time reading books and articles written by marine biologists. Doing so will help you on your path to becoming the marine biologist you want to be. Learning from those who already have the knowledge and the ability you seek to gain is paramount to you becoming what you desire.

Are you spending time with those who are genuinely confident (not just wearing a mask of confidence that you can see right through) and who feed your own confidence? If not, you should be. And before you claim not to know anyone who helps you believe in yourself and feeds your confidence, let me remind you of the easy accessibility of books and podcasts these days. We are no longer forced to walk five miles to the closest library. Books, podcasts, videos, etc.

are an avenue to some of the best people in the world who can help you on your journey to greater confidence.

And if you have those around you who are sucking the confidence right out of you, you need to try to distance yourself from them. That's tough if you live under the same roof with someone like that, but you've got to find a way to hear their voice less and hear more from the voices that feed your confidence.

When the time comes for you to battle against the Giant of Self-Doubt, let me ask you: who is your *corner guy*?

I (Blake) once got in a fight with a bully after school. The bully was a year older and much bigger than me. I shouldn't have felt confident facing this deadly middle school foe but I was, because my big brother, Sammy, stood by my side.

Rocky had Mickey. I had Sammy.

Sammy was one of the strongest kids in middle school, and a loyal brother. Bottom line, I had a competent corner guy.

Next time you watch a boxing match, notice what happens after each round. Each round is three to five minutes long, but then comes the most important minute that the fighter will experience: sixty seconds in the corner. More than resting, that minute is used for remembering. When the round ends, the corner guy places himself in between his fighter and the opponent. The placement is not accidental. Eye to eye, the corner guy reminds the fighter who he is and how he has trained for this moment. He patches him up and sends him out.

For me, that was Sammy. For David, that was God Almighty.

STRATEGY #5: POSITIVE TALK

We've all experienced someone saying something negative about us (having flashbacks to school days?). It's also a safe bet that we probably say more negative things about ourselves than anyone else has ever said about us. We've all heard that negative voice in our heads that tells us we can't do something. That can be an all-too-familiar voice for most of us and it's a confidence killer.

There is great power in positivity. A positive mind is a more confident mind. If you're someone who struggles to be positive, you need to put in some effort to try to be so, even if you don't feel like it. If you act more positive you may just begin to feel more positive—and those around you just might as well.

When trying to combat our self-doubt and find the confidence to face the Giant of Self-Doubt, we need to have as much positive talk coming our way as possible. Try these methods:

> We need to make the effort to speak positively to ourselves about our capabilities. Replace your internal "can't" language with "I can" language. Replace "there's no way" with "I deserve this." Replace "someone else should do this" with "God's made me perfect for this."

1. We need to hear from those who will encourage us as we seek out confidence. Maybe you have that one friend who is your biggest fan and always seems to have the right words to motivate you to take a step forward. Speak more often to that person!
2. There are many great books and podcasts out there

that can help you have a more positive outlook on life. Jon Gordon is an example of a great resource for helping you build a more positive mindset.

STRATEGY #6: QUIT COMPARING

Sometimes the best strategy for improvement is to eliminate something that's holding us back. That's the case with this strategy.

Many of you have heard the quote, *"Comparison is the thief of joy,"* said by former president Theodore Roosevelt. It's a valid statement because as we compare ourselves to others we feel are smarter, more attractive, more successful, etc., we can certainly feel less joyous about our current status (think about continually seeing everyone's highlight reels on social media). But not only can comparison rob you of joy, it can kill your confidence.

Goliath issued the challenge for an opponent from the Israelite Army for forty consecutive days without any takers. Speculation would indicate that it's highly likely that each soldier in King Saul's army was guilty of comparing themselves to Goliath. As small as each Israelite was compared to Goliath, they were probably even smaller in their own minds. As they compared themselves to a giant, it was clear they didn't measure up—no single man felt enough against Goliath. Their comparisons killed their confidence and thereby fueled the Giant of Self-Doubt they faced (and would need to overcome before ever facing Goliath).

As we compare ourselves or our situations to others, we often come away with a case of the "nevers." We hear in our heads, "I'll never be as fit as them," "I could never accomplish that," or perhaps, "I'll never have a house like theirs." Instead of finding our Stone of Confidence and putting it to good use, making unfair comparisons is like we're throwing our stone across a lake and watching it skip out of sight.

So if you're someone who would say you struggle with unfairly comparing yourself to others, what can you do about it so that you can feed your confidence rather than starve it? Here are some considerations:

- Take the time to determine the things that trigger you to make unhealthy comparisons that hurt your confidence. Find a way to reduce or eliminate these triggers (yes, this might mean less time on social media).
- Remind yourself of the truth. The truth is that we are all imperfect, despite how perfect someone may appear on the outside; we all have a lot of dirt on the inside that others don't know about. We all have our struggles, sorrows, and regrets. Don't increase yours by comparing.
- When you see how "good" others seem to have it, focus on, and be thankful for, what you have. You might even be able to think of things you possess (non-material things, perhaps) that others wish they had.
- Replace your unhealthy comparison with that which is healthy. Find, follow, and admire those that are doing great things (i.e., being a great parent, an incredible leader, a loyal spouse, a faithful servant for others, etc.). Use comparison to drive you to become more like those who have a great quality of character (and that might not even have an abundance of money or possessions).

STRATEGY #7: DRAW FROM A DEEPER WELL

Till the Spirit is poured on us from on high . . . The fruit of that righteousness will be peace; its effect will be quietness and confidence forever.

—Isaiah 32:15, 17 (NIV)

In our battles against our giants, Jesus wants to operate the sling. We participate in the fight by offering Him our stone. This is what obedience looks like. He will not do that part for us. Jesus then takes the stone, places it in his sling, and with perfection, releases it toward your enemy.

A shallow well is the well of self-sufficiency.

The deeper well is the well of Jesus-dependency.

When we live from an "I got this" place, all the pressure and responsibility sit firmly on our shoulders. We need to live from a place of "God's got this." We still have responsibilities to prepare for the battle, but we rely on the power of Jesus to slay the giant, just as David did. We inaccurately exaggerate this story and think we're David—the ultimate Giant Killer—and we rely on our own dogged determination to defeat our giants.

Friends, *we are not David*. We do not rescue ourselves. We do, however, have a Rescuer by the name of Jesus Christ. He came for your rescue, for your victory. Here is the best news you've ever heard: Jesus is the David for your giant.

This is the good news of the gospel. The water from His well tastes like peace. Its effect is quietness and confidence, and as you drink from that deeper well, there is a phrase in bold on that cup—it reads: **GOD'S GOT THIS.**

With these seven strategies in mind, it's time to experience daring confidence as we take the next step in front of us.

THE GIANT OF ANXIETY

Anxiety and fear are cousins but not twins. Fear sees a threat. Anxiety imagines one.

—Max Lucado
Anxious for Nothing

DISCERN ANXIETY (S2)

FOR MANY READING this book, this giant is your giant.

It's become well documented that anxiety is an American mental health epidemic. It now ranks as the number one issue for women and the number two issue for men.

Statistics tell us that some forty million adults in the United States face this giant on a daily basis. Forty million! This giant is not only reserved for adults either. Twenty-five percent of kids between the ages of thirteen to eighteen are plagued by this, and we believe that number is rising.

Now, before we assume that all anxiety is bad, it might surprise you to know that limited anxiety is actually helpful. We need it to be alerted to danger. As you stand on the curb in rush-hour traffic waiting for your bus, limited anxiety is what keeps you alive. Limited anxiety is not the problem, the problem is when we live in a perpetual state of high alert. That's the problem. Hear us on this, the victory over this giant isn't to never feel anxious, the victory is to not let anxiety govern your life.

Back to the story. *"Then the Philistine said, 'This day I defy the armies of Israel! Give me a man and let us fight each other.' On hearing the Philistine's words, Saul and all the Israelites were dismayed and terrified"* (1 Samuel 17:10–11 (NIV)).

At this point in the story, Goliath hadn't done anything but run his mouth. Day in and day out, he taunted the Israelite Army and instead of saying *"defeat **could** happen,"* they chose to believe *"defeat **would** happen."*

Anxiety does this.

This is why many sports teams lose the game during warm-ups. They see the size and skill of their opponent and believe defeat is inevitable. Like a sports team, we can also allow possibilities to become certainties—not on the field, but in our mind. This is what anxiety does.

Anxiety turns a future possibility into a present certainty.

When we are ruled by our anxiety, we no longer live in the present. We now live in a future that we've become convinced *will* happen. We fill in the unknown with an *assumed* known. We turn a future possibility into a present certainty.

> *Believe nothing you hear, and only one half that you see.*
>
> —Edgar Allen Poe

This quote is deeply helpful when fighting the Giant of Anxiety because there are times we need to believe only some of what we see. That's called limited anxiety. But anxiety believes *everything* it sees, and the truth is, most of what we think will happen, doesn't. Think about how different things would have been for the Israelite Army if they would have believed none of what they heard and half of what they saw? The war likely would have been won (or at least fought) long before David showed up.

As we get familiar with the Giant of Anxiety, it's important to know how it's different from its cousin, the Giant of Fear. They are similar but different. For example, the Giant of Fear is Goliath appearing before the army. They saw the giant. Goliath was not a figment of their imagination—no, he was real. The giant stood there.

The response to the Giant of Fear is, *Whoa!*

The response to the Giant of Anxiety is, *What if?*

- What if this headache doesn't go away?
- What if I don't appear successful?
- What if my kid's stomachache is something more serious?
- What if this lump isn't just a lump?
- What if the boss wants to meet with me because he's going to fire me?
- What if I let the shareholders down?
- What if I don't get into that school?
- What if she's the one, or what if she's not the one?
- What if it doesn't get better?
- What if no one shows up?
- What if this book is a flop?

What if, what if, what if, what if, and by the way, the "what if" weighs a lot! It's like the giant has left the valley and is now sitting on your chest.

In talking with friends, who love Jesus and want to faithfully follow Him, they often arrive at the false conclusion that anxiety is a sin. This adds to the weight that is already there. If that's you, please read this next statement a few times: *Anxiety is a signal, not a sin.*

Let us explain.

How many of you have had a moment while driving your car where the detestable check engine light suddenly appeared? I (Jon) think I'd rather have all four tires blow out than have that wicked light come on. I feel like it taunts me. I can't prove this, but I do think that little light enjoys the havoc it wreaks on my mind. I was so enjoying this drive and then *BAM!* out of nowhere, this happens.

A few months ago, that snarky check engine light came on. I tried to not look at it, but of course, that only worked for a few minutes, so I had to adjust my strategy. I then did something I'm embarrassed to admit. I peeled off my non-transparent oil change sticker and placed it over the light. It felt great for a few weeks, that is, until my transmission literally blew up! I guess I should have paid attention to the light after all.

Anxiety is like that. It's a signal that something must be tended to.

Some of you are choosing to face this Giant of Anxiety, and if that's you, we applaud you. Keep toeing the line. Others, you are placing stickers over the signal and we both know that "sticker" isn't working.

You've been using the sticker of staying busy, or the sticker of numbing with a substance, or the sticker of defeat. You are now agreeing with the giant and learning to live with the giant so much so that he's moved in. This is an obvious statement, but let us remind you, giants take up *a lot of room*. They start in the entryway, move into the living room, and before you know it, they've taken over every room in your house. They no longer live with us, we now live with them. When giants move in, like Cousin Eddy, they don't plan to leave.

For those of you applying "stickers," it's time to trade in that sticker for a stone.

DISCOVER SURRENDER (S3)

All to Jesus I surrender,
All to Him I freely give;
I will ever love and trust Him,
In His presence daily live.

—Judson W. Van DeVenter

SURRENDER SOUNDS PASSIVE until you choose it. In reality, surrendering "all" is one of the bravest and most active things we can do. Something deep within us wants to do the opposite: control. If we rewrote that famous hymn for how we actually live, it would read, "*Some* to Jesus I surrender."

All too often, we resist surrender yet welcome control.

We do this for many reasons. When we have control, we hedge the potential of being hurt again, or at least we think we do. The song we end up writing with our life is titled "I Control All," and that song does not end well. That way of living leads to a white-knuckled existence. What if you were to replace control with surrender?

You might be familiar with a prayer that has helped many experience the freedom of surrender. It's called the Serenity Prayer.

It goes like this: *"God grant me the serenity to accept the things I cannot change, courage to change the things I can, and wisdom to know the difference."*

We love the Serenity Prayer. We find it deeply helpful in choosing the Stone of Surrender but let us be clear on who you are surrendering to and who you are *not* surrendering to.

You are *not* surrendering to the giant.

You are surrendering to the Giant Killer.

As we continue to say, **Jesus is the David for your giant**. This is why we take all of life and surrender it to Him. Our great Shepherd King is looking and longing for you to bring to him your Stone of Surrender.

As Charles Spurgeon once said, *"Our anxiety does not empty tomorrow of its sorrows, but only empties today of its strength."*

You are a Giant Killer, but your victory is a vicarious one. We live *through* Christ who gives us strength.

If you've ever been to a youth sports game, you've seen dads display how to vicariously live through their kids. Dads line the sideline, vicariously living through little Joey or Jane. In fact, we humans all live vicariously through something. If it's not little Joey or Jane, it might be your big corner office, or your degrees, or your status. Living vicariously through something isn't the issue, the issue is who it is we're living through.

Then Saul dressed David in his own tunic. He put a coat of armor on him and a bronze helmet on his head. David fastened on his sword over the tunic and tried walking around, because he was not used to them.

"I cannot go in these," he said to Saul, "because I am not used to them." So he took them off. Then he took his staff in his hand, chose five smooth stones from the stream, put them in the pouch of his shepherd's bag and, with his sling in his hand, approached the Philistine (1 Samuel 17:38–40 (NIV)).

David was presented with the opportunity to advance through the armor of someone else. What a picture of living vicariously through the *wrong* thing. In wisdom, David took off the armor that did not belong to him. He instead chose to *surrender all* and live through the power of God.

The Stone of Surrender we're asking you to find is, in one way, simple. It's doing what you already know how to do: live vicariously through another. You already live vicariously through people and things; we're just asking you to stop living through the things of this earth and to live through Jesus. The wisdom of surrender is that we wisely live through the One whose Name is Victory. As we surrender daily or even hourly, we discover the path that leads to life and victory. In the third verse of "I surrender all," it says, *"May I know Thy power divine."*

Will you choose to head down to the stream again? Reach into the river and choose the Stone of Surrender? Hand all of life over to Jesus? If so, stand back and watch, because your giant is about to fall.

DEVELOP SURRENDER (S4)

WE THINK IT'S important to note that many people experience anxiety on a somewhat regular basis. Others, however, might experience anxiety every minute of every day. Our training and experience have geared us to help those who might struggle with anxiety at times. Others who might have an anxiety disorder should seek professional help. The last thing we want to do is minimize your struggle or offer strategies that leave you feeling more defeated. Mental health is a major issue for many people today. If you struggle with anxiety, you are not alone nor should you try to go at this alone. Please surround yourself with skilled and loving people who can help you walk in victory, minute by minute, and hour by hour.

Often in our work, we are referring friends to Christian counselors and gifted therapists who can help at a much deeper level than the strategies outlined below. With that said, we've provided the following strategies that you can practice on your own to help you find your Stone of Surrender.

STRATEGY #1: JOURNAL YOUR GRATITUDE

We find this stone, in part, through the practice of writing what we are grateful for. Again, the emphasis here is on the word "practice." Just as a baseball player or golfer trains their swing through repetition to develop muscle memory, we train our mind through the repetition of listing out our blessings.

A few years ago, I (Jon) started using *The Five Minute Journal*. This journal has now sold over five hundred thousand copies because it works, in less than five minutes! Every morning and night you practice the power of gratitude. You literally write down a few things you're thankful for.

One of the great thinkers of our time said, *"When I started counting my blessings, my whole life turned around."*

You know who said that? *Dr.* Willie Nelson. If Willie said it, it's gotta be true!

Practicing gratitude can help lessen anxiety by taking your focus from the "what if" to the good that has already come to pass.

STRATEGY #2: HAND IT OVER TO GOD IN PRAYER *WITH* THANKSGIVING

Philippians 4:6 (NIV) has become the number one highlighted verse, according to a few sources. Given how anxiety is a cultural epidemic, it makes sense why.

Do not be anxious about anything, but in every situation, by prayer and petition, with thanksgiving, present your requests to God.

We have a lot of requests that mean so much to us. Often, those requests have to do with relationships or possible issues on the horizon. Those possible issues often turn into the "what ifs." These thoughts begin to fill our minds and anxiety takes over. Instead of allowing those "what ifs" to swirl in your mind, take out a piece of paper and make these thoughts visible. Write them out, one by one.

In the book *Cleaning Up Your Mental Mess*, Dr. Caroline Leaf concludes that *"writing brings order out of chaos by putting your brain on paper."*

The research is substantial. Replace worry with writing. Get your thoughts out of your head and onto paper. This forces us to become conscious of that which is occupying our minds. Once you're done writing out your anxious thoughts, place that piece of paper inside your Bible.

#GodsGotThis.

By physically placing our anxious thoughts in our Bible, we are actively giving those thoughts to God in prayer and petition. This exercise moves prayer from a mental thing to a physical thing. It's a powerful strategy of "presenting our requests to God."

STRATEGY #3: FILTER YOUR THOUGHTS

Remember when the Brita water filter became a thing? It gained such popularity that everyone seemed to have one. You'd fill that baby up with your "dirty" tap water and voilà! Filtered water. The bad stuff would be filtered out. It was the filter that made Brita such a successful product. Its power was found in its filter.

Just as Brita is a great filter for your water, Philippians 4:8 is a great filter for your mind. The next time you are feeling anxious, take that anxious thought and filter it through this truth:

> *Finally, brothers and sisters, whatever is true, whatever is noble, whatever is right, whatever is pure, whatever is lovely, whatever is admirable—if anything is excellent or praiseworthy—**think** about such things.*

> —Philippians 4:8 (NIV)

Let this verse be your thought filter. If a thought you're having is not true, noble, right, pure, lovely, admirable, excellent, or praiseworthy, it needs to get filtered out. Is it easy? No. Does it take practice? Yes. You'll likely need to use this filter repeatedly throughout your day—every day. But the more you do it, the easier it becomes. The easier it becomes, the more successful you will become at keeping anxious thoughts from your mind.

THE GIANT OF TEMPTATION

There's always free cheese in a mousetrap.

DISCERN TEMPTATION (S2)

THE IRISH POET Oscar Wilde honestly quipped when saying *"I can resist anything except temptation."* We're sure the pints didn't help, but at least he's honest.

Temptations are countless and highly personal. Temptations are desires that lead us to do things that are wrong, unwise, destructive, unhealthy, and, often, contrary to the things we actually want to do. We Christians would say simply, *Temptation leads us to sin.* As Christians, we believe that the Giant of Temptation that we face is merely a synonym for Satan.

Satan seeks to destroy us through the lies he tells us, and many of those lies are in the form of temptations. And Satan's lies are as old as, well, the third chapter of the first book of the Bible. In Genesis 3, Satan used temptation to lie to Adam and Eve. Satan tempted them by making them believe they could be all-knowing, like God, if they ate the forbidden fruit. We all know how that turned out.

Temptation comes in many forms, but in this section, we'll focus on *sexual* temptation. Yikes! Many of you will be tempted (no pun intended) to skip the rest of this section and head to the next. For many, this particular Giant of Temptation brings up feelings you'd rather not face. We're addressing sexual temptation because of the prevalence it has in our society and how often we see this temptation lead to the demise of jobs, marriages, and families.

We find it both interesting and telling how David could defeat Goliath but not Bathsheba (more on her in just a bit). David was able to resist the attacks of wild bears, lions, and enemy nations, but when it came to sexual temptation, his ability to resist fell short.

For many of us, the greatest pain and regret in our life is connected to us giving in to sexual temptation (or perhaps the continual giving into it). For many, we're still managing the aftermath it caused or is causing. It all started so subtly perhaps. It was just harmless flirting. It was just a quick glance at that website. It was just talking business over lunch. We never dreamed it would lead to where it led, and it ended up costing us everything.

Temptation typically starts small and appears harmless because Satan knows that we wouldn't likely fall for the trap if he revealed all his cards at the start. If we could see into the future and see all the damage that would result, we'd likely never take the bait. A fish would never bite the hook if it could see the frying pan waiting on the shore. But when it comes to sexual temptation, we are often so mesmerized by the bait Satan places on the hook, we are blind to the consequences of sinking our teeth into it.

It's been said before that *"sin will take you further than you want to go, keep you longer than you want to stay, and cost you more than you want to pay."* The irony of this quote is that it was written by a leader whose legacy is forever tarnished due to the Giant of Temptation. A great example of how we should practice what we preach.

Before you skip to the next section, hear us on this: we are against **condemnation,** but we are for **conviction**.

Condemning isn't how we roll. Condemnation leads to shame, and shame leads to further hiding, and further hiding leads to further sin, and further sin leads to further pain. Condemnation gives your Giant of Temptation more power, but conviction is different. Conviction is the outcome of truth received. Conviction reveals where we are falling short in hopes that we'll right the ship. Conviction leads to further freedom, and further freedom leads to further joy. We hope this section convicts you if needed.

We all have a past here. More than that, we all have a future, and our hope and prayer is that your future is filled with a whole lot more freedom and a whole lot less regret when it comes to sexual temptations.

We must discern temptation accurately. Pastor Erwin Lutzer said it so well when he said, *"Temptation is not a sin; it is a call to battle."*

In the city of London, during World War II, they experimented with something called the air-raid siren. The siren was a strategy to alert the British people that an attack was on the way. It reminded them to take cover for the battle that was now at hand. In this section we're sounding the siren, alerting you, perhaps awakening you, to take cover in the strength of God. Don't look to your own strength when it comes to battling sexual temptation. Our human strength often falls short.

As we discern sexual temptation (S2) in this section, we'll look at the two most prevalent forms that it takes today.

THE FORBIDDEN FRUIT

David was on top of his game. His victory over Goliath catapulted him into celebrity status. They began to sing songs about him and slowly but surely, victory after victory placed David as king. It's true that we are vulnerable in the valleys of life. David knew all about these valleys, but it's also true that we are vulnerable on the mountaintop.

Question: When did David fall?

When you study David's life, you will find that he fell not in the canyon, but in the castle.

David traveled through many canyon experiences, and as he did, he seemed to grow more aware of God and more aware of his own shortcomings. The canyons were some of his best seasons of faithfulness. How is it that once David was in the "castle," he would commit a sin, then a crime, that would tarnish his legacy? Did he think he was untouchable? Had he convinced himself that he deserved anything he desired, even another man's wife?

David had muted the alert siren but turned up the volume of his sensuality in the form of a woman named Bathsheba he happened to see bathing from the palace rooftop. While his soldiers were away, engaged in battle, David himself was about to be in the fight of a lifetime. You can read about it in 2 Samuel 11.

The truth is, the Giant of Temptation only engages us in

battle when it knows we are vulnerable to its lies (unfortunately, most of us are vulnerable most of the time). If the giant knows it doesn't stand a chance against us, it won't waste its time—it'll pick on someone else.

David wasn't vulnerable to sexual temptation in those canyon experiences. Why? In those times of his life, David was clinging to God for mere survival, and there simply wasn't room for sexual temptations because of his proximity to God. God was meeting his needs, and when we're close to God and relying on Him, the less likely we are to listen to the lies of Satan and look to anything or anyone other than God to meet our needs.

David *was* vulnerable to the Giant of Temptation in the castle, however. Why? Scripture doesn't outright tell us, but we can make a couple of good guesses.

One, would Bathsheba even have been an option for David if he weren't the king? Sure, we're told in 1 Samuel 16:12 that David was handsome, but would Bathsheba have even given him a second look during one of his canyon experiences? Our guess is no. We're all more attracted to people who've found some measure of success and seem to have it together. The clout and status that comes with being king made David much more likely to face sexual temptation because he simply would have had more options than a commoner would in his day. If you find yourself in the "castle" or on the mountaintop of success, you need to be on high alert! Listen for the sirens! The Giant of Temptation has no problem fighting at altitude!

The second, and likely the biggest reason David was more vulnerable in the castle, was that he'd let down his guard. Perhaps, he didn't need God in his castle days to the degree he needed God in his canyon days. Maybe he lost a little humility and began taking credit for his own successes. Perhaps, he lost some of his proximity to God, and as a result, felt a little lonely one particular evening. Instead of surrounding himself with people who would protect him from such temptations, he had men around him that helped him pursue the temptation (2 Samuel 11:4). Just the slightest bit of letting his guard down provided the enemy an opportunity.

The Giant of Temptation seized the moment in the form of Bathsheba, wife of Uriah. Instead of running to God to satisfy his loneliness, David made a late-night booty call. With that call, he put himself in a position to fall. And fall he did.

When our guards go down, our vulnerability to attack goes up. God wants to use our vulnerability to draw us to Him, leading to our victory. Satan wants to use our vulnerability to make us easy prey for destruction. When we are feeling vulnerable, we must seek God's help with all we have in those moments. Failing to do so opens us up to attacks.

THAT FOUR-LETTER WORD

For you, it may not be someone's spouse that tempts you, but it's *that* website. Screens have become one of the greatest tools of Satan in the history of time. We're not against technology. Tech has done some wonderful things. We love being able to Facetime with family when we travel and to find a quick how-to video to fix something around the house. There are some good things about it, but now *porn is in your pocket*. And porn might just be the worst four-letter word of them all.

When we were growing up, you had to go to the store or pay off your older buddy to buy a pornographic magazine. Porn was not easily accessible for most. Now, it's readily available on your phone—24/7. Technology has created a gale behind the back of this Giant of Temptation. He was big before 2007, but now, his size seems immeasurable.

Here are some disheartening stats regarding pornography:

- 64 percent of Christian men and 15 percent of Christian women view pornography monthly.
- 79 percent of Christian men between the ages of 18–29 view porn monthly.
- 65 percent of young men and 18 percent of young women watch porn weekly.
- 56 percent of divorce proceedings cite pornography as one of the reasons for the divorce.

Pastor Craig Groeschel says this of sexual sin: *"It fascinates then it assassinates."* Unfortunately, far too many people are being fascinated and assassinated by porn. Maybe it started with simple curiosity, or you thought it might spice up your marriage, but then you found yourself drawn to it time and time again like a moth to a flame. You started turning to porn when you felt lonely, when you felt unworthy, when your sexual advances toward your spouse were turned down, when you were anxious or feeling stressed. You now use it to medicate all sorts of uncomfortable emotions. The size of this giant in your life has grown into what some would even call an addiction.

Porn is a lie. It wants you to think it can help solve your problems, make you feel better, and enhance your love life, but those are lies. Porn does the opposite of what it promises.

It causes more problems (in marriages, relationships, careers); it makes you feel shame and guilt, and causes you to lose sexual interest in the spouse you've pledged your devotion to. We need to stop believing the lies that porn promotes.

DISCOVER TRUTH (S3)

We are either in the process of resisting God's truth or in the process of being shaped and molded by his truth.

—Charles Stanley

WHETHER YOU COME face-to-face with sexual temptation through a forbidden relationship or through pornography, you need help when facing that giant. Since we know the Giant of Temptation, a.k.a. Satan, is using lies as his weapon against us, we need to use the one stone that can defeat lies. We need the Stone of Truth.

Of all the stones we mention in this book, this stone might be the most ambiguous. You might be wondering, "What is truth and how do we discover it?" Valid questions. Truth comes in so many forms. Imagine going to the stream like David to find the Stone of Truth but instead of finding one, you find a hundred of them, but only one will work against the giant you're facing. You must choose the right truth for the lie you're hearing and the temptation you're being told you should give in to. We've got to uncover the lie we are hearing in order to find the Stone of Truth we need.

The Bible tells us Satan is the father of lies (John 8:44) and it also provides us with the truth to combat his lies. Let me (Blake) give you an example of how I rely on the Stone of Truth when I hear Satan's lies and am tempted.

The biggest lie that Satan has led me to believe in my life is that I am a reject. And yes, this is a result of the split of my family as a child and other experiences since then. Because I've struggled with this lie throughout my life, when I'm feeling rejected, the Giant of Temptation usually appears and whispers something like this in my ear, "The emotions you are feeling really suck! You would feel better (even feel accepted) if you had a couple drinks, or eat that box of Oreos, or look at porn." See what we mean when we say temptations equal lies? None of these temptations are going to provide any lasting relief from my negative emotions and will actually make me feel even worse (because of shame) if I do give in to the temptation.

So, when facing the Giant of Temptation, I have to find the right Stone of Truth to take into battle. I look to the Bible for a Stone of Truth that will rebuke the lie ("I am a reject") that is leading to the temptation. I've done word searches in the Bible ("the truth") that I can read to remind me of the truth that I am actually a *chosen* child of God. God has not rejected me, he has chosen me! So if I am feeling rejected, cast aside, or just plain unworthy, I pull out my phone and read this rebuke that I've created from scripture:

> *I'm not rejected. In fact, God has chosen me and given me important work to do (John 15:16). He even*

set me apart before I was born (Jeremiah 1:5). He chooses to be with me, strengthen me, and help me. I'm His chosen servant and He has not rejected me (Isaiah 41:9-10).

What is the lie you might be believing that is making you susceptible to the Giant of Temptation? Discover that, and then you can turn to the Bible to discover the particular Stone of Truth you need most.

DEVELOP TRUTH (S4)

BEFORE WE LAY out some practical strategies to battle against sexual temptations, we must start by stating that a proactive approach is the best approach when it comes to the Giant of Temptation. In fact, we believe that if you are proactively pursuing your relationship with God, then you'll likely face fewer temptations, and when you do, you'll be better prepared to handle them. Furthermore, if you neglect your relationship with God, you will likely never have lasting victory over sexual temptations. That's where the first strategy comes in:

STRATEGY #1: DRAW NEAR TO GOD

Can you imagine the strength we would have to battle temptations if God was always near to us—like He was near to David when he faced Goliath? James 4:8 says that when we draw near to God, He will draw near to us. Did you hear that? You don't have to do all the work. A great relationship takes two putting in the effort. It's impossible to have a close relationship with anyone if only one person is putting in the work. So, what are you doing to draw near to God?

Maybe think about what you've done over your lifetime to develop a relationship with your best friend. Drawing near to God might look similar. Our guess is that you've probably spent a lot of time with your best friend. You've spent time getting to know them. You've probably made them a priority in your life. You've likely opened up to them and shared with them your struggles. And you probably do these things consistently, not just every once in a while. Should drawing near to God not be similar?

Are you prioritizing spending time with God to get to know Him as you would a best friend? Are you praying (talking) to Him? Are you going to Him with your struggles? Are you reading the Bible and perhaps memorizing it to get to know Him better? And are you doing these things consistently?

The best strategy to defeat any temptation is to be so closely aligned with God that you are always under His protection—you haven't ventured off trying to do things in your own strength. Prayer, worship, Bible reading and study, scripture memorization, quiet meditation, journaling, walks in nature, and Christian mentoring are just some of the things you can do to draw near to God. Doing things like these—consistently, not just when you feel like it—are the key to a life of greater victory over sexual temptations (and all temptations for that matter)!

This strategy is *the* most important in this section (and hey, for all giants we face). The rest of these strategies are things you can do to help prevent sexual temptations from occurring, or to help you resist them when they appear. They can prove helpful in the fight, but we believe that only God can provide you with lasting victory when it comes to sexual temptation. If you're not willing to give this first strategy the time and effort it needs, the rest of these strategies are like bailing water out of a bottomless boat.

STRATEGY #2: LOCATION, LOCATION, LOCATION

If you ask a real estate expert how to succeed in purchasing a property, they will say, "location, location, location." When it comes to fighting the sexual variant of the Giant of Temptation, we want you to use that same saying. Here's why: sexual sin is 90 percent location.

It's hard to have an affair with them if you refuse to have lunch with them.

It's hard to cross physical boundaries with them if you refuse to get horizontal.

It's hard to look at porn on your phone at night if your phone is never in your bedroom.

It's hard to watch that dirty movie if the only TV is in the family room.

See what we are getting at? Be strategic. Practice placing yourself (or your technology) in a location where you can resist and win. Those who demonstrate the most self-control are those who have to call upon it the least. Thank you, James Clear, for that life-changing insight.

Think about it. What if you made sexual temptation as inconvenient as possible? If your issue is what you're streaming on TV, take your TV down and put it in the closet or garage. I promise you, you'll watch less TV. If your issue is that social media platform you're scrolling through on your phone, delete those apps or leave your phone in your kid's room at night.

Why are you playing games with this? Be vigilant. Stop putting yourself in a position to fail. Be smart! Think *location, location, location,* and watch your giant fall.

STRATEGY #3: URGE SURFING

Temptation often comes in waves. A Christian therapist once said we should practice "urge surfing." It's said that most urges last under thirty seconds. If you can fight the urge for thirty seconds, you may just defeat the current wave of temptation you're feeling. Oftentimes we feel overwhelmed by the wave of temptation and think we must fight for an hour, that we might as well give in to the temptation because the urge will never dissipate.

Practice thirty seconds of faithfulness at a time.

Set a timer on your phone. Text a friend and tell them you're riding the wave of temptation. Perhaps you can pray during the urge and ask for God's help. See how you feel five minutes later. The urge will diminish.

Now yells louder, but later lasts longer.

—Levi Lusko

Invest in your future marriage. Invest in what's later, because later is longer. Now, it yells. It makes a scene. It's an intense wave and it always promises what it can never deliver, but you can ride the wave instead of having it crash on you.

Surf's up!

STRATEGY #4: UPROOT IT

Some of you may have had the unpleasant experience of taking down a giant, unwanted tree or large shrub in your yard. That experience is like practicing self-control when tempted. It takes both time and a lot of help to uproot something that's been there for that long.

If you've struggled for years with sexual temptations, please get Christian counseling. Please! A gifted counselor can help you pinpoint the root that drives you to give in to the temptation time and time again. Identifying the root is critical. The trauma we previously experienced in life is often the culprit.

Perhaps you went through a traumatic experience as a child, and somewhere along the way, you learned that medicating your emotional pain with sexual sin provides a little relief. The problem is the medication just helps momentarily with the symptoms of your trauma; it doesn't bring healing. Thus, you may continually seek out porn, strip clubs, affairs, etc. just looking for a little more medicine. We know people who've been medicating their own wounds for decades with sexual sins and failed to find the healing they need to overcome the temptations.

Thomas À Kempis nailed it when he said, "*The man who only shuns temptations outwardly and does not uproot them will make little progress; indeed they will quickly return, more violent than before."*

Therapy can help you get to the root of the problem and help you find lasting healing. Both of us have done years of therapy to reveal the root of the lies we have individually believed in life. Through that hard work we've found tremendous healing, and so can you.

STRATEGY #5: IRON SHARPENS IRON

King David had men around him who helped him sleep with another man's wife. To have success over sexual temptation, you need to avoid such people. Avoid the coworkers who go out to the strip club after work. Avoid spending time with those you know are cheating on their spouses with disregard of the consequences. You need to have those in your corner who are going to help hold you accountable to a higher standard of sexual purity.

Is there someone you can open up to about the sexual temptations you face and succumb to? Someone you can trust and not shame you? Such partnerships can prove helpful as long as complete honesty and transparency are present. We've heard stories of accountability partners who were more of a hindrance to each other's purity than they were a help. We need someone we can trust and who wants to help us find the victory over the temptation we so desperately desire.

A great accountability partner is someone you will, at times, *really* dislike. Plato was right when he said, *"No one is more hated than he who speaks the truth."* The best accountability partner speaks the truth at all costs. Too much is on the line to do otherwise. A great accountability partner speaks truth, but also helps to make sure we have set boundaries in place to reduce the chance that we take temptation's bait. We've heard stories of accountability partners setting up software and passwords on devices to help their friends remain free. *We love that!* These friends can act as a lifeline you can call when feeling tempted and hopefully help you through the urges.

We both work in a church and are intentional about setting up boundaries to prevent not just sexual temptations but the mere appearance that a sexual impropriety could take place. Some of the boundaries we set up and the standards we hold each other accountable to may seem over the top to some, but they do their job—they protect us! If you are really chasing after sexual purity, there are plenty of boundaries you can establish, but we also recommend a trusted friend who can help you in your efforts.

THE GIANT
OF PRIDE

**If I had only one
sermon to preach,
it would be a sermon
against Pride.**

—G. K. Chesterton

DISCERNING PRIDE (S2)

As I (Jon) write this chapter it happens to be Christmas morning. I'm up early, it's quiet, just me and the lit tree. The timing does not seem coincidental. The single greatest day in history is when God came to us, in a borrowed barn, born to poor teenagers. I know you know the story but think about that. The greatest day in history is also the humblest day in history. Are those two things connected? We believe so.

Of all the ways our all-powerful King Jesus could have entered our reality, he chose the humblest of entrances known to man.

> *Today in the town of David, a Savior has been born to you; he is the Messiah, the Lord.*
>
> —Luke 2:11 (NIV)

St. Augustine once said, *"It was pride that changed angels into devils."* He's right. That is our belief in how Satan and his crew found themselves getting booted from Heaven.

Rewind the tape and you will see pride at every massive personal collapse.

With every affair, pride is there.

With every verbal attack, pride is there.

With every splinter in unity, pride is there.

With every organizational debacle, pride is there.

The Giant of Pride must be recognized and resisted. As long as you have flesh, you will face this deadly foe. Like many giants, this one keeps getting back up. This has been the case forever. The Giant of Pride has been around since the beginning. It defeated Lucifer, demoralized King Saul, and has sidelined more leaders than one can count. Of all the giants in this book, if you lead something, this is *your giant*!

In Jim Collins's book, *How the Mighty Fall*, he does a deep dive, studying companies that were once on top of the world in their industry but unexpectedly declined into oblivion. Their crash was both massive and shocking. For this project, Collins's team focused their work on researching sixty corporations, dating back seventy-plus years. In the end, they found eleven cases that *"met rigorous rise-and-fall criteria at some point in their history."* Jim and his team were able to provide five stages of decline that each of these corporations experienced. If you've yet to read this book, order it now. Spoiler alert: guess what stage began the decline for these companies? You guessed it. Pride.

Jim defines it as *"hubris born of success."*

The proud read this and say, *It happened to them, but it won't happen to me.*

Okay, so you're more gifted? You're more educated? Think about the caliber of leadership that was once leading companies such as Zenith, Hewlett-Packard, and Circuit City just to name a few. Some of the most gifted leaders on the planet were at the helm. They were educated, proven, and successful. The only issue was they knew it. They read their own press. It was at their pinnacle when they were most vulnerable to fall, and fall they did.

Proverbs teach us that *"Pride goes before destruction, a haughty spirit before a fall."*

Lay Jim Collins's work over the story of David. We've focused our attention on the moment when David defeated Goliath. What a highlight reel moment that was! Hold that moment in your mind as you fast forward David's story to when he crashed and burned. If you keep reading David's story, you will eventually get to the point when he is King of Israel. At this moment in his life, everyone either wanted to be him or be with him. David was no longer laying underneath the stars or hiding for his life in caves; at this moment, David is living high on the hill, experiencing success after success as a king. It's in this season of success David takes another man's wife as his own. Her name was Bathsheba. That night, David would sleep with another man's wife. Not only that, but in an attempt to cover it up, David has her husband killed in battle.

Crash.

When I study and compare the victory over Goliath and the collapse with Bathsheba, I see it . . . do you?

David was strongest as a nobody.

David was weakest as a somebody.

Success should be appropriately feared. Instead, pride lures us to celebrate success, crave it, and in the end, take all the credit for it. Hear me on this: pride left unchecked or unnoticed is the quickest way for you to destroy your life and everything you've spent your life building.

A few years ago, I was in the early days of starting Mission Church here in the suburbs of Chicago. We hadn't begun our weekend services yet, so I was able to spend my time team-building, fundraising, and learning from incredible senior pastors like Mike Breaux, Jimmy Seibert, the Ferguson brothers, and Mark Jobe. Men I want to become like. I remember many breakfasts and lunches with some generous pastors who agreed to meet with me. One breakfast comes to mind I will never forget. In hindsight, it has become one of the most important meetings I've ever had.

I was about to sit down with the senior pastor of one of the largest churches in the country. His ministry *was* worldwide and, somehow, I was able to get breakfast with him. It's the equivalent of a young entrepreneur sitting down with Elon Musk. I was nervous yet hungry to learn. About thirty minutes into eating, he asked me, "Jon, what do you think will bring about the manifest presence of God?" *Wow, what a question!* I thought.

I looked at my bacon, then my hashbrowns, as a way to stall. I was nervous to answer. My palms began to sweat. This guy was an evangelical giant. What if I said the wrong thing? What if this was a test? What if he told everyone I was an idiot and unable to start or lead a church? All these questions flashed through my mind, and then I blurted out what I believed and what I continue to believe.

My response: **humility**.

What happened next was shocking. In a crowded yet quiet restaurant, he made the loudest *wrong answer noise* you could ever imagine. You know the buzzer sound on *Family Feud* when you get the wrong answer? Yeah, that sound. It was so loud. People were now looking at me. He followed up that sound with the loud statement: "Wrong answer, try again."

I was so embarrassed—face red, stomach in knots. Not even my bacon could help me in this moment. I did not try again.

For the next fifteen minutes, he made me feel dumb, small, and completely inept. What a gift, right? I now thank God for that experience. In a painful way, I encountered a leader I never want to become *yet* am totally capable of becoming. With enough success, anyone can become that. With enough applause, anyone can be tempted into thinking "they did it." No one is immune to the deception of pride. No one.

It was less than eight years from that moment that this man's ministry collapsed. The crash was loud, painful, yet totally avoidable.

So should we try not to succeed? Is the answer to pursue mediocrity? Not at all. The answer is to recognize and resist pride by practicing humility.

If **pride** is your giant, **humility** is your stone.

DISCOVER HUMILITY (S3)

Pride is your greatest enemy, humility is your greatest friend.

—John R. W. Stott

SEVERAL YEARS AGO, I (Jon) sat in a packed auditorium at the Global Leadership Summit and listened to a talk by an Aussie named John Dickson. His speech was flawless but more than that, it was prophetic. The room needed to hear it. The guy sitting in my chair especially. I've never forgotten this talk. John explained his thoughts about how the greatest leaders of all time had the ability to "hold their power for the wellbeing of others . . .

In his book, *Humilitas,* John Dickson defines humility as *"the noble choice to forgo your status, deploy your resources, and use your influence for the good of others before yourself."*

In my humble opinion, that's the best definition of humility I've come across.

If you want to be a Giant Killer, humility is a **choice** but not an **option**.

In *Humilitas,* John Dickson tells some great stories of humility in action. The first is the story of Sir Edmund Hillary. If that name is familiar, it is because Sir Edmund and his climbing partner, Tenzing Norgay, were the first to summit Mt. Everest. Hillary was later knighted and became famous across the globe. He was thought of as the greatest mountaineer of that day. Dickson tells the following story to illustrate the humble spirit of this great man:

> *On one of his many trips back to the Himalayas, he was spotted by a group of tourist climbers. They begged for a photo with the great man, and Hillary agreed. They handed him an ice pick so he would look the part and set up for the photograph. Just then, another climber passed the group and, not recognizing the man at the center, strode up to Hillary and said, "Excuse me, that's not how you hold an ice pick. Let me show you." Everyone stood around in amazed silence as Hillary thanked the man, let him adjust the pick, and happily went on with the photograph.*

Dickson goes on to tell another story about another historical figure you'll recognize:

> *Three young men hopped on a bus in Detroit in the 1930s and tried to pick a fight with a lone man sitting at the back of the vehicle. They insulted him. He didn't respond. They turned up the heat of the insults. He said nothing. Eventually, the stranger stood up. He was bigger than they had estimated from his seated position—much bigger. He reached into his pocket, handed them his business card, and walked off the bus and then on his way. As the bus drove on, the young men gathered around the card to*

read the words: Joe Louis. Boxer. They had just tried to pick a fight with the man who would be Heavy-weight Boxing Champion of the World from 1937 to 1949, the number one boxer of all time, according to the International Boxing Research Organization.

How did Sir Edmund Hillary and the Brown Bomber respond like this? Simple—they knew who they were. Hillary and Louis could forgo their status because they already had a status.

As you discover humility, know this: humility starts **high**.

This is what C. S. Lewis was getting at when he defined humility as *"Not thinking less of yourself, but thinking of yourself less."*

If you start by belittling yourself, you will become less ready to live with actual humility. You may gain the appearance of humility, but not its substance. On the contrary, when you begin by knowing *who you are*, you aren't looking for the next accolade or next achievement to define you. No, you've already been defined. This is why we can actually do *"nothing out of selfish ambition."* We're not trying to be somebody; according to God, we're already somebody!

When you know *who you are*, you don't need to fear feedback or bash those who disagree with you either. When you know who you are, you no longer feel the urge to somehow feel superior to someone else.

The humble know they are highly esteemed by God. The humble know that on them, the favor of God rests. The humble know that they are joint heirs with Jesus. You can't forgo a status unless you first have a status. Some may call it self-esteem; we call it identity. We have been called Sons and Daughters of God.

> *See what great love the Father has lavished on us, that we should be called children of God! And that is what we **are**!*

> —1 John 3:1 (NIV)

What a status this is!

We are the children of God, and as God's children, we leave the house every day not looking for a status—no, we have a status. The pressure's off. There's nothing to prove. It's an amazing day when you realize you have been freed up to love and serve everyone.

Humility starts high **but stays low.**

A few years ago, my wife bought me the best birthday gift of all time: a dog. I (Jon) love my dog, Jack. He's a pointer, bred for hunting, which I am deeply grateful for. With this, however, comes the daily requirement of exercise. Just about every day, I take Jack on a hike to a nearby forest preserve where Jack gets in his miles. It's nothing out of the ordinary for him to run four to six miles but with that comes the need for water. It didn't take long for Jack to figure out the key to living: water. I've now witnessed Jack on many occasions do what the proud rarely do. Jack leaves the high ground and heads to the valley. Why? If he stays on the high ground, he stays thirsty.

**Jack knows that water runs
to the *lowest* places.**

The creek isn't on the high ground, it's down in the valley. The water runs to the lowest places. The proud stay thirsty, the humble get refreshed.

There's a cost to staying low but there is even a greater pay-off—water, soul refreshment, victory.

> *The Lord takes delight in his people; he crowns the humble with victory.*
>
> —Psalm 149:4 (NIV))

Humility starts high but stays low.

DEVELOP HUMILITY (S4)

DID THE STORIES of Sir Edmund Hillary and Joe Louis decrease their greatness or increase their greatness? Exactly! With those stories in mind, let's practice humility.

STRATEGY #1: PRACTICE SECRECY

How often do you do things on purpose that no one sees? Our guess is not very often. Being seen or recognized is not inherently wrong, it's not how you cultivate more humility in your life. This practice has been around for centuries among those looking to resist pride while deepening their humility.

- What if you were to pull your neighbor's trash cans back from the curb for them before they returned home from work?
- What if you were to give an anonymous gift to a single parent in your community?
- What if you mowed your neighbor's lawn while they're on vacation?

- What if you washed the dishes without standing there waiting for applause?

Bill Gaultiere of Soul Shepherding explains the power of secrecy: *"Secrecy is a discipline of abstinence or self-denial. Denying ourselves attention and praise is a powerful practice for soul transformation. It's a way to help us get free of people-pleasing and managing what people think of us. It makes space for a deeper engagement of love and dependence upon God."*

STRATEGY #2: LEAD WITH CURIOSITY

One of the reasons pride destroys our life and leadership is because the proud often stop learning. It's hard to teach something to someone who already knows everything. Some of you who are further along in your career know when your greatest season of learning was as a rookie. When you first began your craft, you were constantly curious. Your hunger to learn was insatiable. You woke up every day knowing one thing: I don't know enough. Isn't it interesting how that dissipates over time? If we're the smartest person in the room, we need to find some new rooms. The humble practice the posture of curiosity and as they do, they keep getting better.

In his must-read book, *Good to Great*, Jim Collins discovered that level five leaders *"display a powerful mixture of personal **humility** and indomitable will."*

We've had the privilege of being around a few level-five leaders in our lives. Every single one of them made us feel like the smartest person in the room. They asked us more questions than we asked them and the whole purpose of the meeting was for us to learn from them!

One of the best ways to practice curiosity is by memorizing this phrase: *"Wow, that's interesting. Tell me more."* This phrase keeps judgment at bay and unleashes learning.

STRATEGY #3: ASK FOR FEEDBACK

The proudest are the most insecure. Too much is at stake for them to receive feedback, let alone request it. On the contrary, the humble hunt for feedback. They eat it up.

In the book *Thanks for the Feedback*, authors Sheila Heen and Douglas Stone offer three types of feedback that must be utilized: evaluation, coaching, and appreciation.

As for **evaluation**, they say it *"rates you against standards and peers. It lets you know where you stand."* When it comes to **coaching**, *"this information helps you get better and learn. It is an engine for learning."* The final form of feedback is **appreciation**. We hear from leaders all the time who share how they don't feel appreciated or share the famous maxim of how leadership is lonely at the top. It's true, leadership is lonely at the top but, oftentimes, lonelier than it needs to be. Practicing humility in the form of feedback helps leaders feel more appreciated. This is critical. Humility works *for* you, not against you. It can be terrifying to allow others to hold up the mirror but at the same time deeply meaningful. Set a calendar reminder—do whatever you have to do to make this systematized. Humility, in the form of feedback, is something to be practiced over and over again. We all need evaluation, coaching, and the feeling of being appreciated.

In King David's story, after his total blunder and fall from greatness, another opportunity presented itself in the form of feedback. This feedback was deeply painful to receive—

sometimes feedback can be that way. You can read of this in 2 Samuel 12, but the short version is this: The prophet Nathan brought feedback to King David. In the Bible, this was called a rebuke. Sometimes feedback is exactly that. In the end, David humbled himself and received critical feedback that would get him back on track. To us, this was one of David's greatest highlight-reel moments. How many kings would humble themselves like this? Answer: very few.

We want to finish this section by challenging those of you who lead. If you are the leader, you are both a pacesetter and a culture setter. You are.

To the CEO, senior pastor, head coach, superintendent, principal, senator, chairman, or parent: if you want to have an organization that kills the Giant of Pride, this work begins with you.

Show us a prideful leader and we'll show you an unhealthy organization.

Show us a humble leader and we'll show you a healthy organization.

If you're the leader, the most important part of your job is creating and safeguarding culture. Peter Drucker was right when he said, "*culture eats strategy for breakfast.*" The former CEO Mark Fields took it a step further, saying "*organizational culture eats strategy for breakfast, lunch, and dinner.*"

Remember, if you want to be a Giant Killer, humility is a choice but not an option. If you want to be a future level-five leader, make the daily choice to kill pride with the practice of humility. The mighty fell, but they didn't have to fall—they could have chosen a different path. They could have left a legacy worth leaving.

———————

THE GIANT OF LOSS

There is no growth without change, no change without fear or loss, and no loss without pain.

—Rick Warren

Life seems sometimes like nothing more than a series of losses, from beginning to end. That's the given. How you respond to those losses, what you make of what's left, that's the part you have to make up as you go.

—Katharine Weber

DISCERNING LOSS (S2)

WE'VE ALL LOST something—the remote, car keys, our temper. Most of us (if we've lived long enough) have also lost someone, perhaps someone we cared for very deeply. If you don't think this section applies to you at this point in your life, keep this book on a shelf where you can easily find it so you can reference this section in the future. If it hasn't already, the Giant of Loss will find you.

Loss always affects us in some way—often in very deep ways. Unfortunately, loss isn't known for bringing about joy—unless, of course, you're losing that extra weight you've been trying to get rid of.

From the outset, let's be as clear as possible about what the Giant of Loss might look like. Here's a short list:

- Loss of a loved one
- Your team losing the game
- Losing the match
- Losing a job
- Loss of a relationship
- Losing out on an opportunity

- Losing the account
- Loss of your health
- Loss of your wealth
- Loss of safety
- Loss of desire
- Loss of comfort
- Losing your patience
- Losing your identity
- Losing your reputation
- Losing trust in someone
- Others losing trust in you

There are many things we could add to the list, but hopefully you get the point—everyone faces some form of loss regularly.

Although the Giant of Loss is often unmistakably easy to identify, there are times it can be deceptive, appearing in different clothing, trying to elude our "giant awareness" mentioned earlier in the book. Whenever we feel as though we're facing adversity of some type, assume that it could be the Giant of Loss. The adversity may have made us lose our passion, our positivity, our sanity, our sense of security, or a host of other things.

Many people lead lifestyles and have careers that subject them to the Giant of Loss more frequently than others. Health care workers, first responders, military personnel, and professional athletes quickly come to mind. Many of those in sales roles experience loss regularly, as well as business leaders who fail to hit their numbers or have valuable employees who retire or leave to work elsewhere. How important is it for such individuals to be prepared for these battles?

THE GIANT OF LOSS CHANGES YOU

Nobody who experiences significant battles with the Giant of Loss leaves the fight unchanged. This giant deals massive blows that can cut deep, leaving massive wounds in its wake. You will take on damage when you fight this giant. You will be changed from the fight. It's never a question of if you will be changed, but how you will be changed and how much you will be changed.

- A child's parents divorce—that child will be changed.
- A young woman is abused—she will be changed.
- Someone commits suicide—surviving friends and relatives will be changed.
- Infidelity in a marriage—spouses and families will be changed.
- The entrepreneur's company fails—they and their employees will be changed.
- A person loses their sobriety—they and their family will be changed.

Battles with the Giant of Loss can change people significantly. But because all people are different, we can expect that battles with the Giant of Loss will affect people differently. Two people can experience the same type of loss and yet, because of differences in things such as their age, experiences, mindset, and friend group, they can have drastically different reactions to the loss. Not all are changed to the same degree, and although most loss events would be deemed negative, not all people will be changed in a purely negative way. The way we are changed by loss can be as different as the effect boiling water has on the potato and the egg.

The boiling water (like the adversity we face during times of loss) softens the potato, and yet hardens the egg. Battles against the Giant of Loss might weaken some and harden others. Neither are likely the desired results individuals want from the battle, but they are common changes people experience when they are ill-prepared for the battle against the Giant of Loss. Here's a story to illustrate:

> I (Blake) shared a little bit about my birth family in the introduction of this book, but to keep you from turning back, here's an even shorter account. I was born the fourth child to parents who got married right out of high school. My two sisters were the oldest and my brother, Sammy, and I were only separated by thirteen months in age. There was a lot of dysfunction in the family so it was no surprise that my mother and father divorced and the family split up. Sammy and I were sent to live with our great-aunt Martha in a neighboring town.
>
> Now, let's shift our focus to the specific Giant of Loss that Sammy and I faced as toddlers, that we weren't prepared to face—abandonment. Now, maybe it wasn't abandonment in the truest sense of the word (we weren't left on a doorstep under the cover of darkness), but abandonment is what it felt like to us, and therefore abandonment is what it was. Living with Martha was only supposed to be temporary, we were told, but it became permanent. Our mom and sisters wound up moving to Florida and Sammy and I were left behind. I went almost ten years without communicating with them. Our father was completely absent and seemed to have no desire to know his kids—so, yeah, it felt like abandonment.

Sammy and I would be forever changed by the loss, but we were changed in such different ways. In many ways, Sammy was the egg, I was the potato.

Sammy became hardened by the loss. He was often angry at the world it seemed. He had zero respect for Martha's authority in our home. He was often disrespectful at school to both teachers and students alike. He bullied me and my friends who would come visit me at home. As he became a teenager, he had very self-destructive behavior—smoking, alcohol, drugs, fighting, stealing, sneaking out of the house, running away from home, and dropping out of high school. Sammy so desperately wanted the family to be reunited, thinking that would be the answer to his problems. That never happened. Suicide eventually became his escape from the torment he endured.

I, on the other hand, was softened by the loss. I had a huge fear of rejection. I wanted and needed everyone to like me, to approve of me. I found myself acting like a chameleon, changing myself as needed for the audience to ensure I fit in. I let others take advantage of me and my tenderheartedness. I was the consummate people-pleaser. I worked hard at all things I ever did (which led to some success), but it was largely just to try to please or impress others. I thought that if enough people approved of me, then I might just approve of myself. A lot of counseling and learning helped me heal many of the wounds from that early battle against the Giant of Loss.

Two brothers, only thirteen months apart in age, experienced the same loss but with very different outcomes. We can only speculate why. But we know that loss changed them both.

THE GIANT OF LOSS FIGHTS UNFAIRLY

Facing the Giant of Loss is often an unfair battle. Loss can lead to feelings of anger, sorrow, discomfort, fear, self-doubt, medicating in unhealthy ways, anxiety, and more. Did you notice that several of the other giants identified in this book were in the previous sentence? That's because the Giant of Loss can manufacture other giants. That's right, the Giant of Loss can bring other giants into the fight against you, greatly reducing your odds of winning.

Imagine David having to face not just Goliath in that valley, but also Goliath's brother Cletus and his sister Stella—both just as strong and frightening as Goliath himself! What already seemed like an unfair fight would have appeared even more lopsided. (Our money would still be on David, by the way.)

Before facing Goliath, David did kill both the bear and the lion, but he didn't have to kill them both in the same fight! Those were separate battles. If we're not victorious in our battle against the Giant of Loss, we might soon find ourselves fighting against multiple giants at once, hurting our chances of victory.

The Giant of Loss can be like the character in the video game with a cheat code that allows them to have unlimited free lives. You may kill the character over and over again, but they keep coming back, demanding you fight them again.

Fighting the Giant of Loss also reminds us of a famous scene from the 1975 comedy *Monty Python and the Holy Grail*. King Arthur fights the Black Knight and severs his arm off with his sword. Although the Black Knight has clearly been defeated, he replies, "'Tis but a scratch," and wants to continue. The scene continues until the Black Knight has no arms or legs but still is unwilling to admit defeat.

Unfortunately, the Giant of Loss will be an opponent we will face with regularity throughout life. Even David, the original giant killer who went on to become King of Israel, faced plenty of loss. His best friend Jonathan died (1 Samuel 31:2), one of his sons died from an illness (2 Samuel 12: 15–23), and some of his sons betrayed and abandoned him (2 Samuel 15).

Loss is just so incredibly prevalent in life. We cannot escape it. We will face this giant over and over and over. Because of this, our need to be as prepared as possible for such battles is vital.

DISCOVER RESILIENCE (S3)

WHEN WE'RE STEPPING into battle against the Giant of Loss, a battle we will face repeatedly throughout life, we must carry with us the Stone of Resilience.

WHAT IS RESILIENCE?

According to *Merriam-Webster*, resilience is the "ability to recover from or adjust easily to misfortune or change." Misfortune or change are synonyms for the Giant of Loss for many of us.

Since we will face this giant repeatedly, it's important that we're able to recover (hopefully quickly) and adjust as necessary to the new "normal" that loss has brought about. And being resilient means that we will recover and adjust to the new normal that life brings our way as often as we must.

The youth sports world provides a great window into what resilience (and the lack of it) looks like. The resilient kid is the one who can experience misfortune—drop the ball, miss the shot, get penalized, give up a touchdown, lose the match—and bounce right back from that misfortune as if it never happened. The non-resilient kid experiences the same misfortunes and has a difficult time recovering from them. They pout, cry, complain, blame, reduce their effort, or even quit. If you've ever watched youth sports, you've seen the kids described here.

Another way to visualize resilience is to look at a tennis ball hitting a brick wall in slow motion. The force of hitting the wall causes the ball to flatten out like a sugar cookie at Christmas. But of course, almost immediately the ball bounces back to its regular shape as if it had never hit a wall. The tennis ball is resilient.

In this example, the wall is the Giant of Loss, the tennis ball represents us. We are greatly impacted by the wall. We are changed when we hit the wall. Whether or not we're able to bounce back like a tennis ball largely depends on us. Thankfully, we have a brain—the tennis ball isn't so lucky—we should be able to learn from every encounter with the wall so we're better prepared for every encounter going forward, finding its blows less and less damaging.

FINDING THE STONE OF RESILIENCE

When Diana Nyad was nine years old, she stood on the beach in Ft. Lauderdale, Florida, looking for Cuba on the horizon. Her mom told her that Cuba was a little bit too far away to be seen, but that it was so close she could almost swim there. Those words planted a seed inside of Diana that would take root and grow.

Twenty years later, Diana attempted to swim from Cuba to

Florida. And she failed. Diana had an asthma attack while attempting the swim and had to be pulled from the water. After that failed attempt, the dream she had to complete this swim got put on hold. She would do other open-water endurance swims (such as swimming the English Channel) but the swim from Cuba to Florida, which is much longer, got put on hold for a long time.

Diana decided she was ready to try again in 2011. In August of that year, on her second attempt, Diana once again failed to complete the swim. Strong winds and currents and a flare-up of her asthma received the bulk of the blame for this failed attempt.

She attempted the swim a second time that year but had to stop after swimming forty-one hours due to repeated jellyfish stings that caused respiratory distress.

In 2012, Diana once again failed to complete the swim, this time due to strong storms and more jellyfish stings.

Rather than giving up on her dream (which wouldn't make for a story worthy of inclusion in this book), Diana learned from each failed attempt and assembled a team of thirty-five people to assist her in her fifth attempt. In August 2013, Diana and her crew were ready to try again. Special adaptations were made to her wetsuit that would prevent a jellyfish from stinging her again.

Before Diana set out on this fifth attempt, she came up with a three-word mantra to help her in her journey—words that she would repeat to herself as many times as needed during the swim to help her put one stroke after another, after another. The words were, "Find a way." No matter what adversity she faced in the water she was determined to find a way to put one stroke after the next until she completed this dream she'd had for so long.

And on this fifth attempt, Diana Nyad did indeed find a way. She found a way through the sharks, the jellyfish, dehydration, and hallucinations. She found a way to swim 110 miles, over the span of fifty-three consecutive hours of swimming, at the age of sixty-four!

It would have been very easy for Diana Nyad to find an excuse for why she couldn't complete the swim. But instead, Diana chose to find a way. In the process, she provided a great example of what resilience looks like. That ability to face adversity time and time again, learn from the losses, and doggedly try to find a way.

DEVELOP RESILIENCE (S4)

BECAUSE OF THE frequency of our battles against the Giant of Loss, it's imperative that we develop our ability to be resilient in the face of adversity. Resiliency is a skill like any other and it can be developed through practice. Let's take a look at some strategies (both reactive and proactive) that can help us find our Stone of Resilience.

STRATEGY #1: DEVELOP YOUR RESILIENCY REFLEX

Wouldn't it be nice if we were able to instinctively respond to our battles against the Giant of Loss with resiliency? It would be like having a resiliency reflex—it just appears automatically when you need it. Well, we believe a resiliency reflex is something you can develop. It's based on a reactive approach to the small battles you face regularly, to proactively prepare you for the big battles. Here's how.

Our responses to the battles against the Giant of Loss strongly influence the quality of life we enjoy afterward. Think about it—our responses influence the outcomes we get in this life. When you get cut off while driving, your response will determine whether or not that event lands you on the six o'clock news. When your spouse fails to include you in an important decision, your response could determine whether or not you end up sleeping on the couch that night. When your boss asks you to do a task outside of your job description, your response will influence your boss's ability to trust you in the future.

Most events we face in life will be followed by a response from us, which means we get plenty of practice opportunities to build a resiliency reflex. When the events in life are positive (i.e., birthday, graduation, getting engaged, earning a promotion, etc.), quality responses come easier, don't require resiliency, and have less impact on our future. But when challenging or adverse events happen in our lives, it can be much more difficult to have a response that will help provide us with a positive outcome. But it's the quality of the response we have in these challenging moments of loss that is vital to us being able to fling that Stone of Resilience and defeat the Giant of Loss.

Maybe you and others have come to expect our current reflex when faced with adversity, just like the doctor expects our lower leg to jump when they hit us with a mallet below the kneecap. The current reflex might be fear, rage, avoidance, shutting down, or self-medicating in some way. If our current reflexive response is not generating a desired outcome, we have to work to change our response. So, what does it look like to practice developing a resilience reflex? Glad you asked.

In the challenging events that happen throughout our day, we need to practice being intentional about our responses.

This is most important when the event stirs emotion in us, such as anger, fear, or disappointment. We need to learn to do two things well when developing our resilience reflex: (1) pause and (2) ponder.

We need to pause when we are hit with an event that affects us negatively. We can't just respond at that very moment without first pausing to help us gain control of our response. During the pause, we then ponder the possible outcomes of our gut response. In this brief reflection time, if we determine that our initial gut response is not going to generate an outcome we want then we ponder a different response that could possibly generate a better outcome.

So, when an employee is late again, or the report card is bad, or a stranger disrespects you, pause to give your gut reaction a chance to take a back seat to some thoughtful consideration of potential outcomes. Practicing this activity regularly helps to develop resiliency by giving you control over your responses. With enough practice, your resiliency reflex begins to show up instead of any negative reflexive responses we might otherwise have. When we have control over our responses, we are much more likely to show resilience in battles against the Giant of Loss.

The pause-and-ponder strategy is not something we should just spend a day or two on; it's a practice you should adopt for the rest of your life. During each day, we'll likely have many opportunities to use this strategy in smaller battles we face—the dog pooped on the carpet, the kid spilled the juice. When we consistently stack up small wins against small battles that test us, we'll be better prepared for a big battle against the Giant of Loss.

STRATEGY #2: GRIEVE THE LOSS

Blessed are those who mourn, for they shall be comforted.

—Matthew 5:4 (NIV)

Losses need to be fully (not partially) grieved in order to move past the emotional trauma they cause. If your grief is not completed, it will be repeated. How long does that take? Who knows! It takes as long as it takes. Everyone is different and we are affected by every situation differently. But we can't just bury the feelings from the loss deep inside and try to move on, because eventually, the feelings will resurrect themselves in some way, maybe even years later.

Grieving is a process designed by God to help us overcome the hurt caused by the Giant of Loss. This process, when done completely, can also develop our Stone of Resilience, which will help us in future battles with loss. Ever hear about the shortest verse in the Bible? John 11:34 simply says, *"Jesus wept."* Why was Jesus weeping? Glad you asked! Jesus was weeping because his dear friend Lazarus had died. So yes, even Jesus modeled grieving for us.

There are likely hundreds of great books you can find on grief and the grieving process. You may need to invest in one or more of them. Some of us may need to invest time and money into professional counseling to help us navigate the grieving process to help win a battle against the Giant of Loss.

As someone who has dealt with great loss, I (Blake) can share a few things I and others I know have done to help me grieve those I've lost. These could be considered strategies within this strategy and are all geared toward getting emotions out instead of trying to bottle them up and perhaps act as though the devastating loss didn't happen.

- **Speak of the person when they come to mind.** Talk with others about why the person was so special to you and others. Share fun memories you have of them and what you miss about them.
- **Write about them.** Even if you never share what you write with anyone else, the process of writing about your loss helps in the grieving process. Writing about my loss in this book has helped me.
- **Memorialize them.** On the anniversary of the loss, or the other special days you now have to experience without the special person you lost, do something to honor them. There are countless ways to do this (including the two mentioned above).
  o Do something they would love to do if they were with you.
  o Visit their resting place.
  o Talk to them as if they were with you.
  o Gather with others who loved them to celebrate their life on earth.
  o Travel to that special place you shared with them.
  o Watch their favorite movie.
  o Write them a note, put it in a helium balloon, and launch it.

STRATEGY #3: DO HARD THINGS REGULARLY

Since resilience is a skill we need to rely on during difficult times, it makes sense that we would practice this skill by doing difficult things. This means instead of waiting for difficult situations to arise, we either manufacture them or seek them out consistently. Doing so gives us opportunities to practice how we respond in difficult situations and thereby become more mentally tough.

Here are some ideas of how you might do this:

- Wake up and start your day (every day) earlier than usual.
- Take cold showers or baths with some regularity.
- Do workouts that really challenge you physically.
- Participate in events that challenge you, such as 5K runs, half marathons, full marathons, triathlons, obstacle-course races, etc.
- Journal at the beginning or end of each day.
- Have the uncomfortable conversation that you've been avoiding.
- Deprive yourself of that item in your diet that you may over-indulge on.
- Go out of your way to speak to strangers (kindly, of course).

We're all different, so if some of these don't challenge you, find ones that do. The key is to consistently find things that challenge you physically and mentally. This helps develop resilience that you need to rely on when the Giant of Loss appears. Doing hard things also helps you develop your confidence, another stone that's good to have in your sling when facing giants.

STRATEGY #4: LEAN INTO COMMUNITY

This is less of a strategy about developing resilience and

more about leaning into the resilience of others when facing significant loss.

When we face the Giant of Loss, we need to make every effort to do so in a community with others who can help us win the battle. Just as an antelope separated from the herd is more likely to become prey, we are more vulnerable to the Giant of Loss when we are separated from our community. There is strength in numbers. Surround yourself with others who have a sling and stones.

Sometimes when people face the Giant of Loss, they choose to pull away from their community, which may feel like the right decision to them at the time, but it's detrimental to their chances of killing their giant. They go through a messy divorce and feel they've lost credibility. They've made a decision that has caused others to lose trust in them. They've sinned and gotten caught and think others can't forgive them. It's common to see people pull away from their community when these things happen. We need to lean in.

Part of leaning into a community is accepting help from the community. There are so many people who find so much joy in helping others and supporting others through battles with the Giant of Loss. We need to be willing to lean into such people, not pull away from them. If others find joy through showing love and support in our battles, we rob them of that joy if we give them a stiff arm. So let them pray over you. Let them bring you meals. Let them clean your house. Let them help you financially.

Philippians 4:14 tells us it's good for others to share in our troubles. Don't miss that. When you allow others to share in your troubles, it's not just good for you, but it's good for them also. A win-win! Not only can we learn and grow from our battles, but when we lean into others and give them a glimpse into the battle, we give them an opportunity to learn and grow as well.

You've likely heard the statement, "Share the love." Well, share the hurt too.

STRATEGY #5: HAVING HOPE

People with great resilience all seem to have the mindset that brighter days are ahead. They have a sense of hope about the future, no matter how bleak their present may seem. With this type of optimistic mindset, they are better equipped to be resilient when misfortune or change comes.

There's a great chance that when you were in school you experienced two types of days. Some days (maybe not many, but at least a few) you were filled with some level of excitement and anticipation about going to school. You had hope that the day was going to be special. Maybe it was the first day of school, the day of the big field trip, or the day they were serving your favorite lunch in the cafeteria.

Other days were filled with dread about attending school. You just knew it was going to be another miserable day. Maybe you found your classes boring, you had a big test you weren't prepared for, or you knew you'd be facing your bully. Nothing could convince you that there was any reason to be positive about the school day that lay ahead.

Similarly, when people face giants, we often see these two different mindsets appear. The people who choose the negative mindset more often lose the battles. It's almost like they're handing victory to their giant without even putting up a fight. The resilient ones always seem to have hope that things will get better, that things will turn around and work out for the best. They have hope, perhaps a strong belief, that they can defeat the giant in front of them.

What's your typical mindset when you're facing one of your giants? Is your mindset helping you or hurting you in the battle?

We'd be remiss here if we failed to mention that many people have a sense of hope because of their relationship with Jesus. Their faith in Jesus provides them a sense of hope for their future. They firmly believe that God wants what's best for them and that going through difficult situations might just be what's best for them at that time. People of faith often have confidence that when they face giants, like David did, God will help them in the battle, giving them the upper hand.

We referenced 1 Samuel 17:37 (NIV) earlier, when we discussed the Stone of Courage. In that verse, David tells King Saul, *"The Lord who rescued me from the paw of the lion and the paw of the bear will rescue me from the hand of this Philistine."* David's Stone of Resilience was found in his faith. The fact that God had already shown up for him time and time again gave him even more faith. His faith fueled his resilience.

Can you be resilient and not be a person of faith? We think you can. But we also question why you would choose not to lean on a loving father in those times of great need.

EPILOGUE

This is Blake again. Most who know my full story, prior to 2021, would say I've experienced more than my fair share of loss. You've read a bit about those experiences in this book already. In fact, I've been asked on multiple occasions by friends, "How are you the man you are?" These are friends who haven't experienced much loss in life and can't imagine how someone could thrive as I have after all the battles I've been through. But I am not who I am today in spite of what I've suffered through—I am who I am *because of* what I've suffered through. The trials, the pain, the loss, have not been wasted. It's been a critical part of my formation. I am better because of it all.

Jon asked me to close out this book with another part of my story. It's a part of my story that I wish I didn't have to tell. It's been the biggest battle against the Giant of Loss that I've ever faced, and hopefully will ever face.

My wife, Hope, and I were married on June 4, 1994. I was the redneck from Alabama, and she was the Yankee from Chicago. I was the extrovert, and she was the introvert. She came from an intact family; I came from a family that had been blown apart and scattered. Her primary love language was acts of service and mine were physical touch and words of affirmation. We were very different, but we were in love and that, plus God, was all that mattered to us.

Over the years we were blessed with five beautiful kids, three of which were planned! Not every birth came easily, and there were many miscarriages along the way, but we were so blessed to build such an amazing family together.

Hope cheered me on as I worked to climb the corporate ladder for much of my career and she found a way to work and care for our kids, which was especially tough when I had jobs that required a lot of travel. We attended a couple of great churches throughout the years that we loved, and we had a tremendous group of friends. I did well in my business career, and we were able to have our kids attend private schools. Everything was pretty idyllic in our family—until it wasn't.

Hope suffered from rheumatoid arthritis, a disorder of the immune system, which helped explain why she was often sick throughout our marriage. She experienced a lot of painful injections (which caused side effects) over the years to try to slow the progress of the arthritis. On top of that, a few years ago she started seeing a psychiatrist to deal with some unresolved trauma from her childhood. She took several medications to help with insomnia, anxiety, and attention deficit disorder.

Years ago, Hope also stopped attending the church we helped plant years before, insisting she wasn't comfortable there, but never really providing a great reason why. She also began pushing away family members, friends, and even me to a large degree. She isolated herself. She'd come home from work, put on her pajamas, binge-watch

Hallmark movies, and shop on her phone until bedtime. It was like she was trying to escape or medicate her troubles.

More recently, Hope started losing weight uncontrollably. She had suffered from eating disorders before we were married, so I wondered if she was dealing with an old demon. Doctors identified a thyroid issue, but blood work revealed there was likely more going on. Doctors suspected some form of cancer perhaps.

To summarize, Hope wasn't healthy physically, spiritually, mentally, or emotionally. As a result, our relationship certainly wasn't healthy either. Her relationship with God wasn't healthy. Even her relationship with her children, her pride and joy, suffered in some ways.

On the morning of Sunday, March 7, 2021, my wife of twenty-six years took her own life.

Our family has been forever changed. We were devastated, and we're still devastated. She took her life in our own home, which has made remaining in our home a challenge for the kids and me since that dreadful day.

I'd experienced the split of my birth family, the suicide of my brother, numerous miscarriages, the death of friends I grew up with, death of my aunt Martha who raised me (both a mental death due to dementia and later her physical death), but I've never had to face a Giant of Loss of this magnitude.

I'm supposed to face this giant?! Have you seen the size of him?! This isn't a battle I asked for—not a fight I picked. How can I handle life without my wife of twenty-six years, despite our recent struggles? How can I pick up the pieces and carry on?

It was like the Giant of Loss moved into my front yard that day. Just as Goliath, day in and day out, dared one of the Israelites to step up and fight, each day this Giant of Loss dared me to step out into the yard and fight him. And if I was afraid to meet him in the yard, he'd find his way inside my room, staring over me in my bed, daring me to put a foot on the floor.

In the weeks and months after Hope's passing, there were days when I had to wake up and decide whether I was willing to fight the giant. As he stood over my bed and taunted me, I sometimes chose not to engage. There were days when the battle just seemed too big, too overwhelming. The easier choice was to lay in bed and cry, which I did initially.

There have been days since Hope's death where I've felt the most overwhelming feeling of loneliness. The kind of loneliness that makes your stomach hurt, robs you of sleep, drives you to unparalleled depths of sadness, and makes you wonder if you can carry on. I could be in a room filled with my kids and my extended family and yet feel utterly alone.

Even though our relationship was a struggle the last few years, I found myself missing her companionship. I missed having someone I could text during the day with a highlight I wanted to share, to celebrate an accomplishment of one of our kids, or just to check-in. I hated, and still hate, sleeping in a bed alone. Though the distance between us at the end of her life was far greater than our king-size bed would allow, I missed the comfort of being in bed with her.

At times I've wanted nothing more than to run away from

this battle. "Giant, you win. There's no way I can defeat you. You're too much for me." I had no idea how to continue. I didn't know how in the world I would manage to raise our kids without her, how I would manage a household without her, how I would make ends meet without her.

But I didn't run. I didn't consider running away a worthy option. Instead, I chose to face the giant. I've bounced back from adversity a lot in life, and I knew I needed to do it once again—for me and for my kids. There's too much at stake for me to turn tail and run, to avoid the battle like the Israelites did when Goliath challenged them. I found more strength and courage than I knew I had. I received help from others more than I could have dreamed. And I've relied on a number of strategies in this book to help increase the Stone of Resilience needed when facing a giant of this size.

Hope's death has led me to pursue Jesus as I never have before. I've found myself in utter dependence on Him to help me through this. Matthew 6:11 tells us to pray for "daily bread." Boy, have I prayed that a whole lot lately! I find myself wanting weekly, monthly, or even yearly bread, but I've yet to find it. What I have found is that my God gives me what I need each day to get through the obstacles that each day brings. He's given me what I need for the daily battles and I'm trusting Him to repeat that tomorrow.

This book is part of the battle I'm taking to this Giant of Loss. It's part of my Stone of Resilience that I flung at him, which I don't think he saw coming. This book is me choosing to fight the biggest giant I've faced to date. And each day I practice resilience, it becomes easier the next time the Giant of Loss steps forward with his taunts. The Giant Killer in me is alive and well, and it grows stronger with each battle.

So, what about you?

How strong is the Giant Killer in you?

Have you decided to stand and face your Giants?

Will you use what you've learned in this book to equip yourself for the battles to help ensure your victory?

Will you find your Stone of Courage to conquer the Giant of Fear?

Will you find your Stone of Discipline to overcome the Giant of Comfort?

Will you find your Stone of Confidence to defeat the Giant of Self-Doubt?

Will you find your Stone of Surrender to beat the Giant of Anxiety?

Will you find your Stone of Truth to rebuke the Giant of Temptation?

Will you find your Stone of Humility to kill the Giant of Pride?

Will you find your Stone of Resilience to outlast the Giant of Loss?

READ THIS LAST

Throughout this book, we've invited, challenged, equipped, and near 'bout begged you to do all you can to fight the giant that stands in front of you. We believe your giants can fall and must fall. As we wrap this book up, however, there is one giant the Bible speaks of that none of us can fight and experience victory over: the Giant of Sin and Death. Have you considered this giant?

It would break our hearts for you to finish this book and begin to experience victory in the battles of life yet fail to experience victory in the most important battle, the battle of your eternity. Every battle you face is temporary except one, the battle for your eternity.

The bad news is you cannot win this fight.

The good news is you don't have to.

The writer of Hebrews says that we are to *"fix our eyes on Jesus, the author and perfector of our faith"* (Hebrews 12:2 (NIV)).

The two words *author* and *perfector* come from one Greek word: <u>*archegos*</u>.

In the ancient world, when two opposing nations would lock up in battle, as a method of saving men and declaring decisive victory, each nation would choose their own *archegos* to go and fight on behalf of the nation. This tactic should sound familiar. Hint: David and Goliath.

The modern translation of the Greek word *archegos* is the word "champion." The champion would stand in place of every citizen of that nation. He was their representative and substitute.

If he won, they won.

If he lost, they lost.

Every Easter, Christians around the world celebrate the Champion who fought on their behalf. Jesus Christ, our *archegos,* stood in your place and in mine. He fought the giant we never could, the giant of sin and death.

On Friday, He absorbed a death blow, but on Sunday, Jesus, our *archegos*, GOT BACK UP!

The result: we have a **LIVING HOPE** because we have a **LIVING GOD**. Jesus conquered sin and death on our behalf, and because of His victory, we are victorious.

Jesus is the champion. The question is, has Jesus become *your* champion?

Often, we share a simple, yet profound, three-word prayer with folks who are ready to crown Jesus Christ both Lord and Leader of their life.

Jesus, save me.

Imagine all that could happen if you prayed that prayer now?

Imagine what life could feel like if you no longer feared death?

Imagine what life would be like if you knew all your past, present, and future sins were forgiven, forever?

Jesus, save me.

Why not pray this prayer? Why not now?

> *"For God so loved the world that he gave his one and only Son, that whoever believes in him shall not perish but have eternal life."*

—John 3:16 (NIV)

For those of you who choose to *"believe in Him,"* please let us know. We want to celebrate this victory with you and send you some ideas on potential next steps.

Email us at info@giantkillerbook.com

From the bottom of our hearts, thank you for reading this book. We hope and pray it adds value to your life.

Keep working on the five steps of Killing Giants: **Decide, Discern, Discover, Develop,** and **Deploy**.

Here's to a victorious life.

—**Jon & Blake**